BUSINESS, TECHNOLOGY AND FINANCE



# RESTRUCTURING COMPANIES

# METHODS OF IMPROVING EFFICIENCY

# BUSINESS, TECHNOLOGY AND FINANCE

Additional books in this series can be found on Nova's website
under the Series tab.

Additional e-books in this series can be found on Nova's website
under the e-books tab.

BUSINESS, TECHNOLOGY AND FINANCE

# RESTRUCTURING COMPANIES

## METHODS OF IMPROVING EFFICIENCY

ZBIGNIEW KURYŁEK

nova science publishers
New York

**Library of Congress Cataloging-in-Publication Data**

ISBN: 978-1-53613-811-5

*Published by Nova Science Publishers, Inc. † New York*

# CONTENTS

# LIST OF FIGURES

# LIST OF TABLES

# INTRODUCTION

Nowadays, one of the aims of companies is to extend the scope of their activity and reach a better position among the competition on the local and global market. Such actions allow companies to develop rapidly, but may also negatively affect the speed and type of reaction to unexpected economic events. Thus, it may be more difficult to react to the changeability of the environment. In case of expansion to new markets, company value may increase, which, due to a significant capital needed to extend the territory on which the company operates, does not necessarily lead to reaching satisfying financial results. In such a case, the management must react by changing its adopted strategy and improving financial results in a short-time perspective. If there is no improvement, the company's financial situation may worsen. In an exceptional situation, it may also be connected with the loss of liquidity. What is especially important is the time of reaction to a recognized unfavorable financial situation and an attempt to adapt the company to external changes. When the adverse situation is noticed too late or when there is no appropriate reaction, the company may be wound up. Therefore, it is necessary to previously strive for the improvement of internal situation and try to ensure stable operations. The balance in functioning can be reached with theoretical and practical knowledge on the restructuring processes. A proper action plan and selected method of its execution are crucial in making a decision regarding restructuring. The restructuring process is not always a result of a difficult financial situation. It can also be selected due to a need to improve the organizational structure or a situation related to the ownership of the company, and not only the financial results, especially now – in times of numerous acquisitions in many industries. Business entities aim at concentrating their capital and creating capital groups, and a significant share of the market in some industries belongs to several companies. As a consequence, restructuring may be needed to ensure better functioning or improve supervision over extensive entities.

The main theoretical and cognitive objective of this work is a complex analysis of corporate restructuring and its efficiency in Polish business conditions.

The main objective is extended by establishing specific objectives based on factors that are decisive for the introduction of a successful restructuring process, and then the analysis of these factors as key ones for successful restructuring are presented. The following specific objectives are distinguished:

- to specify methods of measuring and increasing company performance
- to analyze the method of conducting the restructuring process,
- to study the influence of restructuring on company finances,
- to specify threats resulting from restructuring,
- to analyze how restructuring is conducted in practice,
- to present advantages and disadvantages of restructuring.

The following research hypothesis has been formulated: Restructuring is a radical method of changing the way a company operates, aiming at reaching a stable level of functioning and then developing a business entity.

The object of research is focused on the restructuring in the context of its influence on further operations of the companies, especially during and after restructuring.

The subject of the research included companies which conducted restructuring in order to improve their difficult financial situation, but also those for which restructuring is a starting point in their further development and remodelling of their current internal situation. The following sources and research methods were used in this monograph:

- the analysis of Polish and foreign academic literature, internet resources, and other sources, including the study of: efficiency measurement and factors, restructuring types and methods, presentation and application of benefits, as well as threats related to restructuring,
- methods of indirect data analysis, which include collection, analysis, description, and proper presentation of data from reporting documents and reports prepared by Wratislavia-Bio Sp. z. o. o. for the presentation of reliable data on restructuring, the way it is conducted, and achieved results,
- methods of comparative analysis of financial results before and after the restructuring process.

The practical importance of this monograph lies in specifying the most important factors as well as crucial aspects and key moments in the process of restructuring, affecting the current and future condition of a company.

The performed analysis, evaluation and drawn conclusions are based on the information and financial data provided by a given company. In case of analysing the possibility of restructuring, the decision is made based on the company's financial, business, and legal condition.

For the purposes of this monograph, financial information provided by Wratislavia-Bio Sp. z. o.o. was used. Then, this work refers to financial reports in order to perform a comparative analysis of real results before, during, and after restructuring. Based on this data, the advantages and threats, as well as conclusions, have been presented.

*Chapter 1*

# Efficiency in Company Operations

## 1.1. Interdisciplinary Character of the Term "Efficiency"

The term "efficiency" or "performance," when referring to company operations, is perceived as an achieved market advantage, but also as the best possible usage of owned resources.[1] Samuelson uses the term "efficiency" to name the usage of social potential to satisfy society's needs and supply for its possible deficiencies.[2]

In the theory of economics, performance is related to an economic development and, as a consequence, to a proper location of property, labor, and production factors.[3]

In organizational studies, efficiency is associated with performance, profitability, effectiveness of operations, but, considering the importance of these terms and prioritizing them, it can be said that efficiency is the most important. Thus, the mentioned words can be treated as a specific method of measuring efficiency.[4]

---

[1] E. Szymańska. 2010. "Efektywność przedsiębiorstw — definiowanie i pomiar." *Roczniki Nauk Rolniczych.* Series G, *Ekonomika Rolnictwa*, V. 97, Z. 2, Warszawa: 152.

[2] P. A. Samuelson, and W. D. Nordhaus. 2007. *Ekonomia*. V. 1. Warszawa: PWN: 329.

[3] N. Acocella. 2002. *Zasady polityki gospodarczej*. Warszawa: PWN: 37.

[4] E. Skrzypek. 2017. "Efektywność ekonomiczna jako ważny czynnik sukcesu organizacji." [In:] T. Dudycz, G. Osbert-Pociecha, and B. Brycz (eds.). *Efektywność – konceptualizacja i*

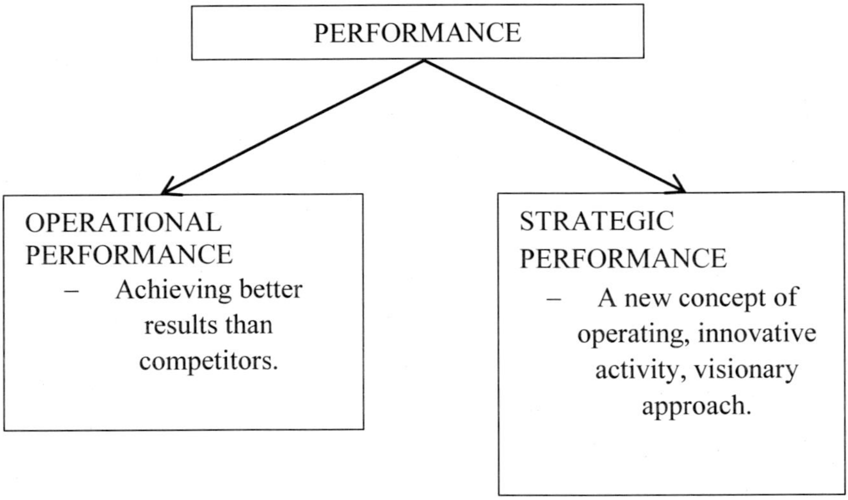


Source: G. Osbert-Pociecha. 2007. "Relacja między efektywnością i elastycznością organizacji." [In:] *Efektywność — Rozważania nad istotą i pomiarem.* Edited by T. Dudycz, Ł. Tomaszewicz. Wrocław: AE Wrocław: 337–349.

Figure 1. Performance in a company.

In general, performance can be divided into operational and strategic performance (Figure 1).

Operational path is based on achieving the best effects in activities similar to those achieved by competitors. Strategic path, in turn, involves designating new methods of operation and determining an innovative direction in company operations in a given sector. It involves implementing solutions and, as a result, achieving outstanding profits in the form of expansion opportunities, possibilities of winning new markets on which the company can operate, or the reduction of business activity costs.

Performance, or efficiency, can thus be defined in different ways, considering[5]:

*uwarunkowania*. Prace Naukowe Uniwersytetu Ekonomicznego we Wrocławiu nr 262, Wrocław: Wydawnictwo UE we Wrocławiu: 314.

5 A. Rutkowska. 2013. "Teoretyczne aspekty efektywności – pojęcie i metody pomiaru." *Zarządzanie i Finanse* no. 1, p. 4, Gdańsk: Uniwersytet Gdański: 440.

- The difference between expected results and incurred expenses; from the perspective of proper functioning of the company, the effects should be at least minimally higher than incurred expenses,
- Efficiency as the effects divided by incurred expenses; if the result is higher than 1, the effects are higher than expenses,
- Efficiency as a return on investment, which includes the division of effects by expenses. It is expressed as a percentage.

Efficiency in a company can be understood as the effectiveness of company operations or economic performance. As such, efficiency shall be analyzed through the goals of companies, which may be diverse.[6] Such diversity determines the multiplicity of dimensions and aspects, as well as an equivocal character of the measurement of efficiency.

Efficiency can have different dimensions[7]:

- Material efficiency – related to the execution of a company mission
- Economic efficiency – aiming at the best usage of sources spent on expenses in order to reach better results
- Technical and manufacturing efficiency – a way of using owned resources
- Environmental efficiency – concentration on the environmental protection and renewable sources of energy
- Quality-based efficiency – relating to efficiency and quality in management
- Social efficiency – corporate social responsibility, which means aiming not only at reaching economic results, but also at improving the way people or environment function
- Ethical and cultural efficiency – creating and promoting ethical and cultural norms in order to allow for the development of companies, but also building a civil society. A society's interest is

---

[6] J. Kulawik (ed). 2008. *Analiza efektywności ekonomicznej i finansowej przedsiębiorstw rolnych powstałych na bazie majątku WRSP*. Warszawa: 7.

[7] A. Jaki. 2012. *Mechanizmy procesu zarządzania wartością przedsiębiorstwa*. Kraków: UE: 128.

to develop and to work towards cultural, economic, and social growth of its region and country.

- Behavioral efficiency – it is focused on actions aiming at promoting the interest of company employees.

Efficiency is also included in the VBM concept (Figure 2), which combines strategic decisions with operational ones. In such a case, the aim is to increase efficiency and, as a result, to grow the value of company, taking into account general directions of development and the usage of management tools in order to reach such objectives as, among others, improving business model, well-functioning internal information, and reporting systems. These elements affect the way company operations are managed and lead to the company reaching its objectives.[8]

Throughout the years, with the increase of knowledge on companies, better access to data, and the development of sciences, new methods and directions in the measurement of company operations were determined.

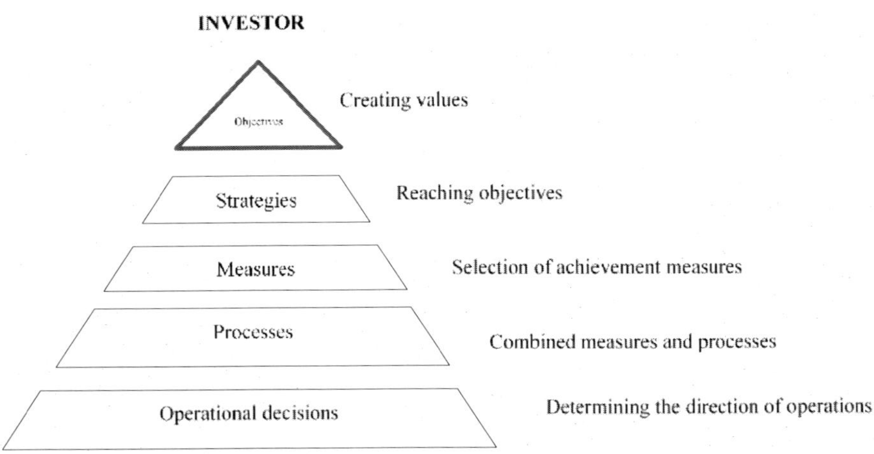


Source: T. Dudycz. 2005. *Zarządzanie wartością przedsiębiorstwa*. Warszawa: PWE: 31.

Figure 2. The concept of VBM.

[8] T. Copeland, T. Koller, J. Murrin. 1997. *Wycena: mierzenie i kształtowanie wartości firm.* WIG PRESS: 87.

Some researchers identify efficiency with profitability, which is justified when financial analysis is treated as a basic context; however, measuring company operations through the perspective of profitability can have several weaknesses, including the following:

- It is an accounting measure, which results from the accounting policy and can be subject to manipulation,
- It refers to the past, so it is focused on a business activity seen in isolation and does not include the effect of environment on a company,
- It leaves out matters related to the risk, dividend policy, or changes in the value of money in time, which can lead to overestimation of reached return rates,
- It does not include capital structure in a company[9].

## 1.2. Factors Affecting Company Efficiency

Company operations are open to cooperation with other entities, which means they are shaped by the environment. As a result of its business activity, every company not only is shaped by its environment, but also affects it to a certain extent.[10] With regard to the level of changeability, there are three types of environments[11]:

- Stable environment – there is a stable and predictable demand for products, and regulatory matters are predictable and easy to apply,
- Changeable environment – changes in the market functioning, demand for products, or regulations take place rapidly, but they do

[9] M. Walczak (ed.). 2003. *Analiza finansowa w zarządzaniu przedsiębiorstwem.* Warszawa: 22.

[10] G. Dorozik. "Identyfikacja czynników prowadzących do sytuacji kryzysowych podmiotów gospodarczych" [In:] L. Dorozik (ed.). 2006. *Restrukturyzacja ekonomiczna przedsiębiorstw w świetle polskiego prawa upadłościowego i naprawczego.* Warszawa: PWE: 17.

[11] J. Penc. 1997. *Strategie zarządzania, perspektywiczne myślenie, systemowe działanie.* Warszawa: Placet: 22-23.

not surprise the management team, which is able to react in a predictable way. Changes continue, but they can be predicted, which allows for a proper adjustment of operations and continuation of the company development,

- Turbulent environment – all elements affecting a company change quickly and tend to be surprising. They happen when there is an unexpected change in the demand for products, when regulations diverting an existing market situation change, or after a technological development which changes the rules of functioning. It is crucial for the managing persons to find a proper strategy in a situation that changes dynamically, under the influence of changes which are hard to predict.

Companies are affected by internal and external factors, and their operations are channelled in three main areas: in the economic, legal, and technical-organizational one. Thus, many different factors can influence a given company and, as a consequence, affect its efficiency. The main factors affecting company operations are as follows[12]:

- Economic conditions
  - National economic situation,
  - Macroeconomic factors and regulations.
- Market
  - Existing competition,
  - Barriers for entering the market,
  - Recognizability and importance of the company and its products,
  - Trends specification and prediction.
- Capital
  - Structure of owned capital,

[12] G. Dorozik. 2006. „Identyfikacja czynników prowadzących do sytuacji kryzysowych podmiotów gospodarczych." [In:] L. Dorozik (ed.). 2006. R*estrukturyzacja ekonomiczna przedsiębiorstw w świetle polskiego prawa upadłościowego i naprawczego*. PWE, Warszawa: PWE: 18.

  - Access to financing,
  - Bank sector stability.
- Raw materials and energy
  - The costs of utilities resulting from the conducted business activity,
  - Raw materials and energy price control,
  - The availability of raw materials.
- Social assets
  - Education level in a country or region in which a given company operates,
  - Professional qualifications and skills of employees,
  - Availability of the management and specialists in a given field,
  - Work ethics.
- Culture
  - Models and rules of behavior,
  - Organizational culture,
  - Value system.
- Political factors
  - Predictable and stable country budget,
  - National debt burden,
  - Transparency of a tax system,
  - Government activities.

In actions aiming at executing the strategy through the company objectives, one important element is budgeting – which originates from ancient Egypt, Greece, and Rome – initially related to the state budget, and then used in corporate finance management. Budgeting constitutes a company's financial plan which includes cash inflow and outflow. Thus, it is a method of internal management of resources aiming at ensuring effective operations and, as a result, leading to the execution of strategic objectives. Budgeting affects[13]:

---

[13] M. Dylewski, B. Filipiak, P. Szczypta. 2010. *Budżetowanie w przedsiębiorstwie. Aspekty rachunkowe, finansowe i zarządcze*. Warszawa: Cedewu: 10.

- planning future activities in a company, which prevents it from making decisions too fast,
- shaping communication and internal control allowing for informing about company opportunities and threats,
- proper management of all processes and tasks, their proper execution by starting with plan implementation, followed by taking actual actions,
- creating an audit system in order to determine all deviations from previously assumed conditions for execution,
- creating a system of evaluating the execution level of tasks and objectives.

Budgeting can lead to the execution of short-term objectives, such as[14]:

- increasing financial liquidity,
- controlling operating results,
- mitigating risk,
- increasing the company value,
- improving the corporate management.

Budgeting can also be used to execute mid-term objectives, such as[15]:

- increasing technological efficiency, introducing innovative solutions, limiting the need for materials,
- ensuring effective and proper cash management,
- reaching the stability of company finances.

Budgeting is a method which requires certain changes in a company, executed in the following areas[16]:

[14] Ibidem: 13.
[15] Ibidem: 14.
[16] Ibidem: 18.

- Work time,
- Accepting and handing over materials, goods, and products,
- Business process management,
- Finance management,
- Conducting internal settlements,
- Communication method and information flow.

Before a budget is prepared, the following tasks should be completed[17]:

- Performing the analysis and review of a company business activity,
- Creating a strategic plan,
- Determining the objectives of company operations,
- Selecting a budgeting method.

Apart from that, a properly formed method should be used to prepare a budget including such elements as[18]:

- Time horizon,
- Strategy execution based on planned income and expenses,
- Revenues and costs,
- Method of information and documents transfer.

The following budgeting methods including expenses may be distinguished[19]:

- Incremental budgeting method,
- Expense planning method based on nature,
- Budget programming,

---

[17] Ibidem: 30.
[18] Ibidem: 19.
[19] G. A. Gianakis, C. P. McCue. 1999. *Local Government Budgeting*. Praeger: 19–38.

- Task-based expense planning,
- Zero-base budgeting,
- Result-based expense planning.

The main problems with budgeting in a business activity can be as follows[20]:

- Poor budget flexibility related to an analytical approach,
- Complicated nature and time needed to execute procedures related to budgeting can lead to overload of the management team,
- Vast or excessive bureaucracy resulting in the increase of the number of archived documents,
- Limited influence of the management or the lack of it, with top-down budgeting.

A company is an element of a bigger whole, such as a macroeconomic system. It is shaped by connections and relations developing in the company's economic environment, which is evaluated in the context of the state of economy. The most important indicators in the measurement of a country's level of development include[21]:

- Growth rate and the return of capital rate,
- Interest rate,
- Employment level and unemployment rate,
- Determining whether there is inflation or deflation and their measurement,
- Economic environment (macro environment),
- Social and cultural factors,

---

[20] E. Hempenstall. 1999. *Being Successful in Budgeting*. Dublin: Blackall Publishing: 147–157.

[21] G. Dorozik. 2006. "Identyfikacja czynników prowadzących do sytuacji kryzysowych podmiotów gospodarczych." [In:] L. Dorozik (ed.). *Restrukturyzacja ekonomiczna przedsiębiorstw w świetle polskiego prawa upadłościowego i naprawczego.* Warszawa: PWE: 23.

- The system of norms, values, and behaviors affecting the hierarchy of satisfying needs, and determining occurring changes (showing current trends, thought-out decisions about the purchase of a product or services, not on an impulse),
- Demographic factors:
  - Society's age structure,
  - The way households are run and managed,
  - Changes in the teenagers' lifestyle,
- Legal factors,
- Political factors.

In macro environment, numerous relations are created, and they can have a direct and indirect influence on the way a company functions. Macro environment can include the following elements[22]:

- Technological,
- Economic,
- Social,
- Demographic,
- Political,
- Legal,
- Cultural, and
- Ecological ones.

When referring to macro environment, we can differentiate the following methods of analysis:

- Methods without scenario[23]:
  - Trend extrapolation methods – this method is based on mathematical models used in forecasting. With the use of

[22] Ibidem: 23.
[23] A. Bitkowska. 2010. "Przebieg procesu restrukturyzacji przedsiębiorstwa." [In:] Bitkowska A. (ed.) *Procesy restrukturyzacji warunkiem poprawy konkurencyjności przedsiębiorstw*. Warszawa: Difin: 159.

recognized measurement methods, it is possible to show future trends without any deep analysis of real conditions,

  - Delphic method (experts' opinions) – in this method, experts' discussion was replaced by special questions prepared in the form of polls. The poll process was divided into several stages. The results are transferred to experts and take part in the next poll stages. When the experts want to change their opinion, they have to provide reasons for such a change. The process of carrying out polls with a Delphic method is executed to the moment of reaching a certain agreement in opinions,
  - Analysis of a strategic loop – this method is based on checking to what extent a currently executed strategy in a company is adapted to its operations and environment. Next, possible changes which can happen in the future in the environment are presented, and their influence on the company is determined,
- Scenario-based methods –
  - Scenarios of possible events – based on creating a list of possible events and processes which can take place. Apart from that, it includes a preparation of a plan of how to adapt to events presented in the list,
  - Simulation scenarios – involving previous evaluation of strategic objectives from the perspective of changes in the environment which can affect the company,
  - Environment state scenarios which include rating and determining to what extent environment factors affect a business entity. What is more, in these scenarios, we determine how likely it is that listed factors occur,
  - Detailed scenarios of environment states – it is necessary to specify strategic and single processes. Methods of creating and executing processes, and especially of increasing process efficiency, are determined.

The environment affects the possibility of sector development. One of the factors are barriers to entering the market. Fewer barriers mean that there are bigger development possibilities. M. E. Porter differentiates the following barriers[24]:

- Economies of scale,
- Capital investments,
- Customer loyalty,
- Distribution channels,
- Localization, patents, availability of materials.

It is important to select competitors from the environment. The following methods can be used in order to recognize the competitors:

- Strategic group mapping – a method in which we list the competitors and determine the position of the company. Competitors can connect in order to reach competitive advantage of strengthening entry barriers or creating obstacles in the implementation of a specific strategy in other companies.
- Point-based evaluation of sector attractiveness – this method allows you to indicate the main characteristics of a given sector, as well as to perform a comparative analysis of sectors. A detailed list of characteristics is related to rating the factors – providing information about which factors are the most important for a given company.
- Experience curve – relating total costs in a company to its production in a long-term period.
- Experience curve is related to the following elements[25]:
- Economies of scale – the increase of production capacities is related to a more beneficial distribution of fixed costs per a production unit, and, as a consequence of the increased production,

[24] A. Koźmiński, W. Piotrowski. 2002. *Zarządzanie. Teoria i praktyka.* Warszawa: PWN: 172–173.

[25] A. Bitkowska. 2010. "Przebieg procesu restrukturyzacji przedsiębiorstwa." [In:] Bitkowska A. (ed.) *Procesy restrukturyzacji warunkiem poprawy konkurencyjności przedsiębiorstw.* Warszawa: Difin: 166.

also negotiations with suppliers and recipients are different and can be more beneficial than before, due to the increase of orders and delivered volumes,

- Specialization – this process allows for a more efficient use of production capacity, based on earlier business experience, which can affect work performance and efficiency,
- Innovations – they do not have to be associated with a completely new, previously unknown product, but they can include modifications of a currently manufactured product, resulting in improvement of this product.

Currently, companies function in a turbulent environment, as academics and business practitioners often call it. Conditions in which companies operate are very dynamic, unstable, and often difficult to predict. What is more, state support is often limited, if it is applicable to big entities due to the scale of their operations and capital intensity. In times of globalization, companies do their business transnationally, thanks to which they gain economic benefits. However, there are also weaknesses of this solution, such as a difficulty of managing a global company, little flexibility in adapting to market changes, or greater product and service standardization, which, on the one hand, leads to a possible bigger sale, increased brand recognizability, and reduction of production costs, but, on the other hand, contributes to the creation of a "global village" with little diversity in the world. Apart from that, it is also necessary to have greater financial resources to spend on business operations in many parts of the world, or at least greater resources for marketing in order to work on brand recognizability.

However, small and medium companies can be game-changers, as they decide on the intensity of national economic growth in different countries. Through their innovative and flexible activity, such companies can work towards a continued growth in the industry. Thus, it is not needed for small companies to compete with big ones, but that joint operations aiming at the development of products, services, and then the sector and, as a result, the whole economy are possible, leading to the creation of the environment which supports starting business cooperation of entities and inspires business initiatives in the society. Forming foundations for supporting business activity can result in the improvement of the country and global economy in the future.

## 1.3. Efficiency and the Aim of Company Operations

Efficiency should be analyzed from various perspectives, considering also how it is affected by company objectives (Figure 3). The selection of measures for evaluating efficiency depends on the objective which is to be achieved. The objectives in business activity can differ depending on the industry, sector, or the specific character of company operations. Apart from these factors, also a time horizon should be taken into consideration, with a focus on short-, mid-, or long-term periods. However, in practice, the time of planning a business activity is usually very short, and the perspective of the management is focused on the monthly, quarterly, and annual summary of their business activity. In special situations, business activity planning goes beyond the time of one year.

Financial efficiency of a company, including its objectives, can be associated with actions aiming at reaching good financial results, allowing to cover all costs incurred before, but also to reach an acceptable return on investment, taking into account to what extent the owners are willing to take risks. Thus, to reach an intended effect, it is necessary to act within certain accepted risk in the context of a possible positive financial result.[26]

In 1980s, the way company objectives were perceived was remodelled by the scientists. Previously, the objectives were perceived through the perspective of efficiency measured based on various indicators. The view of a company was changed, and the focus was shifted to the value of a company and to what causes the increase of this value, based on the concept of management through value[27].[28]

---

[26] A. E. Helfert. 2004. *Techniki analizy finansowej*. Warszawa: PWE: 24.

[27] Value Based Management (VBM)

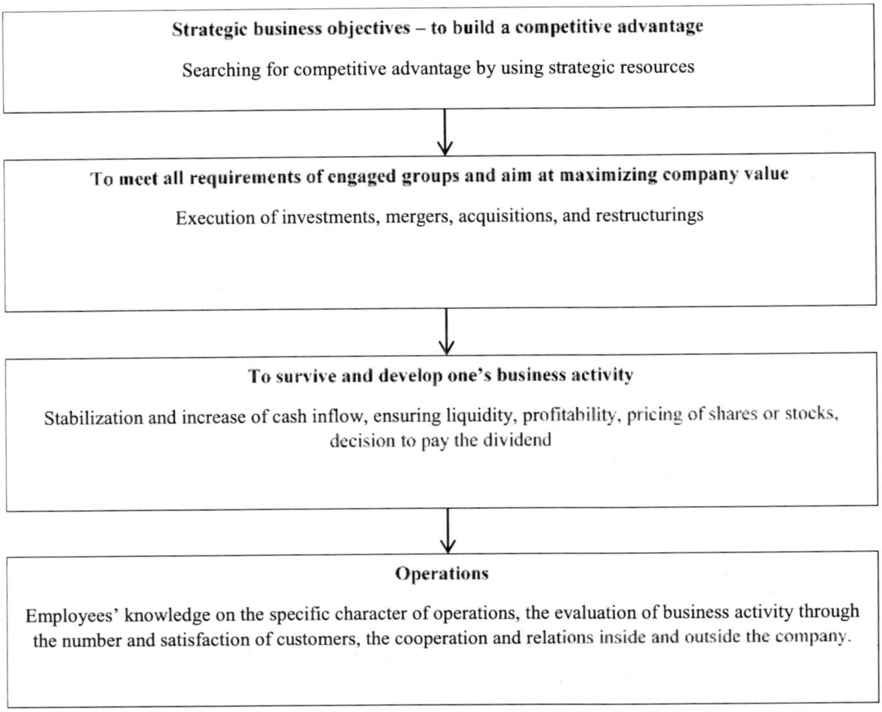


Source: B. Pomykalska, P. Pomykalski. 2008. *Analiza finansowa przedsiębiorstw*. Warszawa: PWN: 20.

Figure 3. The hierarchy of company objectives.

The development of the theory of economics affected the process of company efficiency management and led to the creation of new concepts, techniques, and tools of efficiency increase. The company functioning is improved by setting specific short- and long-term objectives and working towards their execution. The employees perform their work, having in mind the task of achieving a specific objective, and, currently, this objective can be achieved by project execution. By specifying the objective properly and presenting it to the team, we indicate the direction in which the company develops and show the factors which are to decide whether this objective is achieved or not. Objectives in a company sometimes have little in common with one another, especially considering employees' and

---

[28] J. Kulawik, ed. 2008. *Analiza efektywności ekonomicznej i finansowej przedsiębiorstw rolnych powstałych na bazie majątku WRSP*. Warszawa: 9.

owners' objectives. Employees usually aim at reaching short-term benefits, whereas owners – at reaching benefits which they have established for themselves. In fact, objectives can be divided into two groups:

- Economic objectives – maximization of benefits and owned resources
- Social objectives – the way the employees cooperate and work together to achieve a common objective.[29]

In the theory of behaviorism, there are two concepts regarding the objectives of company operations:

- Minimal profit – estimating a minimum level of net result which will satisfy the owners,
- Maximizing an objective – there are many groups in a company, and their objectives may be different, as a result of which the attitude to maximization must be different, as it is impossible to maximize many objectives at the same time. Thus, it important to hierarchize objectives in company operations.[30]

More and more frequently, company operations are based on project execution, with specific priorities given to each project. Thus, the objectives get hierarchized and are divided into main and specific objectives – a group ("bundle") of objectives.

Upon reflection, the aim is to specify the objective of company operations. In general, it results from the nature of company activity – its main objective, including strategic tasks, which include:

- Increasing company value,
- Maintaining or possibly, increasing one's share in the market,

---

[29] T. Rojek. 2016. "Wykorzystanie narzędzi restrukturyzacji w procesie zarządzania efektywnością przedsiębiorstwa." *Studia Oeconomica Posnaniensia*, vol. 4, no. 2. Poznań: UE: 135–154.

[30] Ibidem: 140.

- Achieving planned operating profit or net profit,
- Achieving the planned sales level,
- Achieving the planned territorial reach of one's operations (developing from a local company to operating in the whole country or Europe, or even doing business globally),
- Maintaining and improving the current position among competitors.

The listed objectives can also be ordered based on the division into the main objectives, basic objectives, and sub-objectives (Table 1).

After the main objective is specified, a bundle of specific objectives is determined. Specific objectives are attributed to employee groups created in a company, e.g., in the form of departments. Groups execute projects, and their aim is to work towards efficient execution, which means that specific objectives (a bundle of objectives) are achieved.[31] Specific objectives in individual groups in a company can be divergent. That is why, sometimes, their simultaneous execution can be difficult. Thus, it is important to set a priority of objectives and the order of their execution. For the harmonious development of a company, it is important to have specific objectives which are consistent or have something in common, which leads to an improved efficiency of operations.[32] Achieving specific objectives at different times leads to the execution of a clearly specified main objective. Thus, the organization develops in its chosen direction, specified with its main objective.[33]

Company objectives may also have a normative aspect, which is regulated by acts, constitution provisions, or articles of association. Documents specify the proper way of company functioning in the context of applicable legal standards and adopted rules for business operations.[34]

---

[31] J. Lichtarski (ed.). 2003. *Podstawy nauki o przedsiębiorstwie*. Wrocław: AE: 36.

[32] J. Żurek (ed.). 2007. *Przedsiębiorstwo, Zasady działania, funkcjonowanie, rozwój*. Uniwersytet Gdański: 37.

[33] J. Kortan (ed.). 2009. *Innowacje w strategii rozwoju organizacji w Unii Europejskiej*. Warszawa: Difin: 176.

[34] J. Duraj. 2000. *Podstawy ekonomiki przedsiębiorstwa*. Warszawa: PWE: 54.

**Table 1. Hierarchy of objectives in a company**

| Main objective | Basic objectives | Sub-objectives |
|---|---|---|
| Maximizing owners' wealth | Maximizing balanced profit | Revenues and profits |
| | | Costs and losses |
| | Maintaining financial liquidity | Liquid funds |
| | | Due liabilities |
| | Innovation and development | New products |
| | | Investment in development |
| | Satisfying customer's requirements and needs | Strengthening one's position on the market |
| | | Efficiency of advertisement and marketing |

Source: A. Buczkowska. 2012. "Cele przedsiębiorstwa a pomiar jego dokonań." In: *Zeszyty naukowe Uniwersytetu Szczecińskiego*, no. 684, Finanse, rynki finansowe, ubezpieczenia, no. 45: 9.

Some authors distinguish the following basic company functions[35]:

- a supply (or production) function, which consists in creating and introducing to the market goods and services which satisfy old, traditional needs or needs that have been newly created by the company as a result of its marketing activity. The supply function can thus serve as a function which makes the economy and consumption more advanced;
- a demand function, which companies execute as market participants who report a demand for material and personal factors of production, e.g., the outcomes of work done by other production companies or organizations providing services (banks, insurance institutions);
- a social function, which results from the fact that companies, in their region, affect the social environment in which they function, and their operations are based on cooperation and personal relations, serving as a space of different conflicts and habit

[35] A. Oleksiuk., J. Białek. 2013. *Mikroekonomia*, (ebook). KeyText.

shaping, as well as an environment in which the processes of training and educating employees take place.

A concept of management by objectives (*MBO*) also emerged, listing the most important objectives and determining their importance by granting them significance labels. Such objectives are monitored and analyzed, leading to conclusions and to the strategy of company functioning.

Thus, company efficiency and financing are a strategic objective whose execution is measured based on the effects achieved versus the costs incurred.[36] Efficiency is evaluated based on the assessment of company operations in the past. The evaluation is important for the selection of new directions of development and main objectives which are to be executed in the future.

Thus, in the context of formulating a strategic objective, it is important which strategy a company has adopted. Creating a company strategy affects its development in the future. It is important to base this strategy on a consciously selected concept of operating, based on an adopted model of functioning created as a result of analyzes, calculations, or earlier business experiences. When formulating a strategy, we need to focus on the following elements[37]:

- Current position of the company and its perspective for the future,
- Determining the position in which the company should be in the future,
- Barriers and challenges related to the improvement of the company position in the market,
- Steps that need to be taken to improve the position of the company in the market.

[36] Ibidem: 42.

[37] M. Porada-Rochoń (ed.). 2009. *Restrukturyzacja przedsiębiorstw w procesie adaptacji do współczesnego otoczenia*. Warszawa: Difin: 68.

The factors which decrease the efficiency of company operations, with the deterioration in the agile functioning of the company as a conglomerate are as follows:

- The company has developed rapidly and is a big entity which is difficult in the management process.
- Various organizational units are under pressure to operate almost completely independently, which may distort the direction of company operations,
- Eliminating company units characterized by low profitability or even results that are below the break-even point of the company,
- Increasing the efficiency of executed processes by introducing a new structure, e.g., holding.

The above factors indicate that it is necessary to introduce changes preventing destabilization and to adapt the strategy or strategic objectives to the current or new and previously unknown situation in a given organization.[38]

The company owners have an objective of increasing the entity value. This objective results from the nature of establishing companies which are supposed to bring profits – the increase of value – in a wider perspective. The execution of this objective is related, however, to the task of satisfying market needs by producing goods and providing services. A positive reception of a product or service by the recipients will affect the execution of the main objective of bringing the highest value to the owners. The returns to scale may strengthen maximization of company value expressed with such strategic objectives as: profit growth, sales increase, better position among the competitors, aiming to achieve the main objective of the company founder.

---

[38] P. Maśloch. 2011. *Restrukturyzacja przedsiębiorstw w Polsce w dobie transformacji i globalizacji*. Toruń: WSB Toruń: 112.

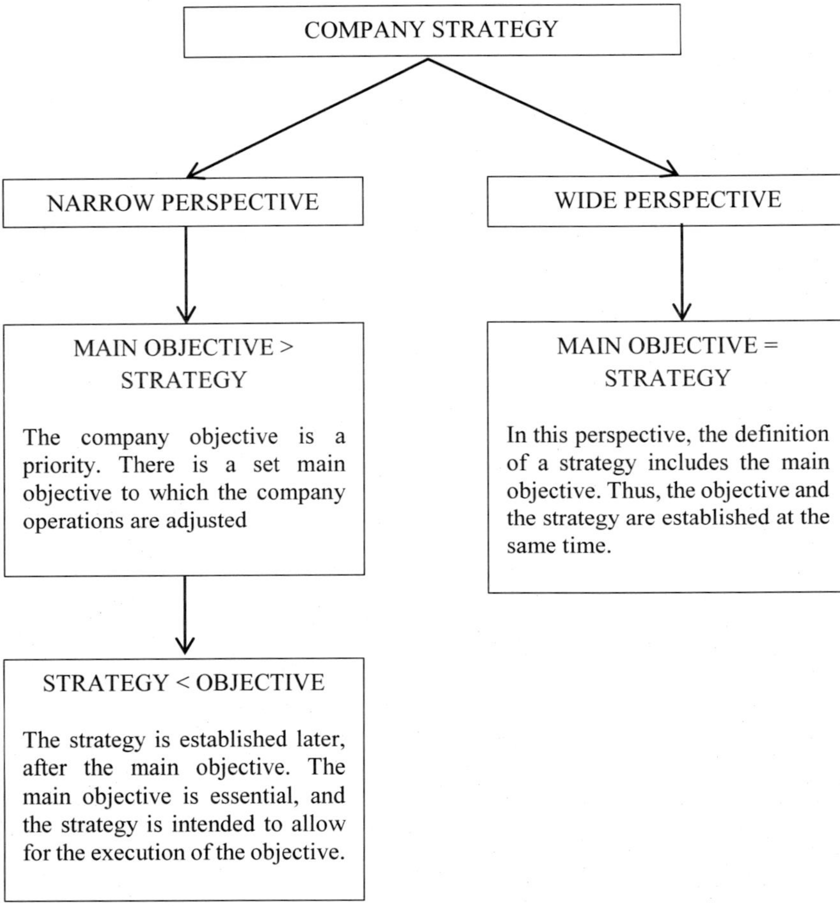


Source: Author's own analysis based on M. Garstka. 2012. *Restrukturyzacja przedsiębiorstwa – podział przez wydzielenie*. 2nd ed., Warszawa: Cedewu: 14.

Figure 4. Company strategy–perspectives to its definition.

There are two main perspectives to defining the company strategy (Figure 4). They are related to the way objectives are formulated and achieved. From the first perspective, the strategy is intended to allow for the achievement of the objective of an external character. First, the objective is formulated, after which the strategy can be created. From the second perspective, defining a strategy involves setting company objectives. A common ground of different perspectives for defining a strategy lays in determining and presenting the way to achieve objectives in a company with owned resources and external factors, such as the environment in which an entity operates.[39]

A strategy has the following characteristics:

- Cooperation – execution of the strategy in the form of cooperation of a group of people in a given area in a company,
- Objective – the task is to achieve a set objective of a company,
- Resources – proper use of resources owned by a company,
- External Factors – the environment in which a company operates.

The strategy should be shaped based not only on the currently owned resources, but also on new resources which can be owned in the predictable future. This means that future actions should be planned properly and the strategy should be updated with the change of company situation or its environment. Set company objectives can be achieved with the use of different decisions and actions, which should not be taken one by one, but as a series of decisions and actions leading to achieving a given objective.[40]

The selection of a proper strategy is crucial for the functioning and growth of a company. The choice of a strategy, its implementation and execution is important for achieving the objective of the company. In general, strategies can have a general form of the following[41]:

- Focusing on the main business activity,
- Different forms of diversification,
- Reduction,
- Winding-up,
- Mixed.

---

[39] M. Garstka. 2012. *Restrukturyzacja przedsiębiorstwa – podział przez wydzielenie*. 2nd ed., Warszawa: Cedewu: 13.

[40] Ibidem, 14.

[41] A. Thompson, A. Strickland. 1984. *Strategic Management,* Business Publications Inc., Piano: 80, qtd. in M. Garstka. 2012. *Restrukturyzacja przedsiębiorstwa – podział przez wydzielenie*, 2nd ed. Warszawa: Cedewu: 15

**Table 2. Company strategies including market attractiveness and the position among the competitors**

| **Strategies of company development** | | **Company position among the competitors** | | |
|---|---|---|---|---|
| | | strong | average | weak |
| Market attractiveness | large | Expansion | Expansion | Selective development |
| | medium | Expansion | Selective development | Benefitting from an achieved market position and abandoning the strategy |
| | small | Selective development | Benefitting from an achieved market position and abandoning the strategy | Benefiting from an achieved market position and abandoning the strategy |

Source: L. Garbarski. 1992. *Marketing*. Warszawa: PWE: 334.

Strategies can be divided into[42]:

- Growth strategies,
- Stabilization strategies,
- Defence strategies,
- Mixed strategies.

The choice of a company strategy is a multi-criteria decision which depends on the owners' or managers' vision for the development of the company at different stages. Also, the time horizon of an applied strategy is important because the short-time perspective can be completely different compared to the long-term one. The choice of a strategy can depend on different factors, including market attractiveness and position among the competitors (Table 2). When specifying market attractiveness and assessing the position among the competitors, it is necessary to prepare a

[42] L. Rue, P. Holland. 1989. *Strategic Management.* New York: McGraw-Hill: 41.

matrix presenting the company growth strategy. Based on these factors, three strategies can be selected:

- Expansion strategy,
- Selective development strategy,
- The strategy of benefiting from an achieved market position and abandoning the applied strategy.

In the selection of a strategy, it is important to choose a proper method of executing company strategy (Figure 5). It is possible to execute company's strategy internally or externally in a more extensive way.

Strategy execution is related to its influence on the company and measured through the efficiency measurement[43]. If the efficiency is not sufficient, it may lead to the introduction of a restructuring process. Connecting the strategy with restructuring can involve several areas[44]:

- The main axle – the strategy is related to the functioning of a company as a whole, whereas restructuring can affect only a part of an organization,
- Principles – the strategy can have a higher priority than restructuring, whereas the opposite situation is multidimensional and depends on the current situation of the company,
- Concept – mission of company may be created outside of the area of restructuring, whereas the restructuring process aims at improving the company situation from a wide perspective,
- Tools – restructuring process is a tool used to execute a strategy. However, there may be situations in which the strategy is less important or completely dominated by the principles of the restructuring process.

---

[43] M. Jablonski. 2017. *Methods of Evaluating the Investment Attractiveness of Business Models in the Context of the Performance Management Concept,* [in:] M. Jablonski, *Strategic Performance Management: New Concepts and Contemporary Trends.* New York: Nova Science Publishers: 1-18.

[44] M. Garstka. 2012. *Restrukturyzacja przedsiębiorstwa – podział przez wydzielenie*, 2$^{nd}$ ed. Warszawa: Cedewu: 16.

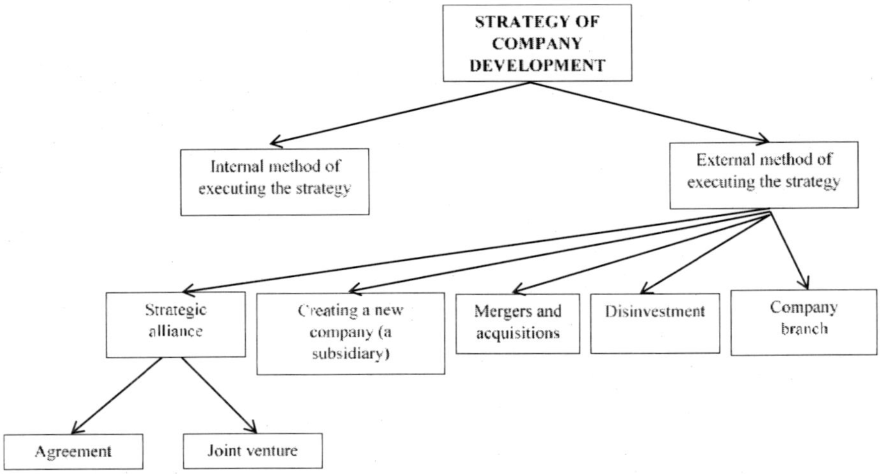


Source: M. Garstka. 2012. *Restrukturyzacja przedsiębiorstwa – podział przez wydzielenie*, 2nd ed. Warszawa: Cedewu: 50.

Figure 5. Methods of executing company strategy.

In company management, it is crucial to determine strategic factors and their characteristics which lead to the execution of the main objective and the company plans. The following strategic factors can be distinguished[45]:

1. Strategic objectives – actions aiming at achieving competitive advantage and striving for the position of the leader, or establishing a stable situation in the industry if a dynamic development is inaccessible,
2. Market definition – diverse product offers are taken into consideration, as well as a wide range of operations including national and international activity, with an increasing focus on a strict specialization of operations,
3. An actual strategy – preparing a strategic activity plan, indicating directions for further development, deadlines for development tasks, and progress verification,

[45] B. Gajdzik. 2012. *Restrukturyzacja przedsiębiorstw w warunkach destabilizacji otoczenia na przykładzie branży hutniczej*. Warszawa: Difin: 132.

4. The way of competing – selecting a way of achieving competitive advantage, actions aiming at company expansion by increasingly innovative operations based on a specific area of activity,
5. Approach to innovation – working towards creating new ways of functioning based on developing current ideas or combining them and creating an original product or service[46]. Such an approach leads to the status of a pioneer and directly affects the company share in the market and the way it is perceived. Apart from that, it is possible to imitate models commonly functioning in the industry, which can, however, bring a lesser outcome than being a pioneer. The examples include such companies as Apple which reached greater prestige as a pioneer in the production of smartphones and became more recognizable on the market than other similar companies. Apple's competitors, such as Samsung, while imitating Apple, also contributed to product development, but their results, especially within first several months or years, were not as significant as the results of the idea originator. From a long-term perspective, a company which is an author of a given idea can become an industry leader by making the product more advanced. Toyota, which produced passenger cars at the beginnings of its operations, focused its activity mostly on following competitors in the car industry, imitating cars produced in the United States by General Motors. Toyota's persistent and step-by-step pursuit, in a long-term time horizon led to the situation in which two Companies compete with each other by selling products worldwide.

In general, company strategies can be ordered based on the criteria of their authors[47]:

---

[46] More about new product strategy can be found in: M. Relich. 2015. *A computational intelligence approach to predicting new product success. Proceedings of the 11th International Conference on Strategic Management and its Support by Information Systems*: 142-150.

[47] Ibidem: 131.

1. Great strategies[48]:
   - Strategy of growth,
   - Strategy of related diversification,
   - Strategy of unrelated diversification,
   - Strategy of reductions,
   - Strategy of stabilization.
2. Corporate strategies[49]:
   - Olympic strategy,
   - Strategy of market expansion,
   - Strategy of purchasing companies,
   - Rescue strategy,
   - Strategy of creating competencies and culture,
   - Strategy of results control.
3. Competition strategies[50]:
   - Differentiation strategy,
   - Cost leadership strategy,
   - Strategy of concentrating on a market niche.
4. Strategy of market position[51]:
   - Strategy of a leader,
   - Strategy of a president,
   - Strategy of a follower,
   - Strategy of a market specialist.

## 1.4. COMPANY EFFICIENCY MEASUREMENT

The process of measuring company operations efficiency was already analyzed in the 19th century, with the peak of research on this topic occurring at the beginning of the 20th century in the US along with the

[48] R. W. Griffin. 2000. *Podstawy zarządzania organizacjami*. Warszawa: PWN: 236.
[49] R. Koch. 1998. *Strategia*. Kraków: PWSB: 106.
[50] M. E. Porter. 1998. *Choix strategiques et concurrence*. Ekonomica, Paryż: 38.
[51] E. Dichtl, O. Issing. 1984. *Exporte als Herausforderung fur die deutsche Wirtschaft*, Deutscher Institute Verlang, Kol.

growth of companies and the accessibility of financial data. Greater access to information and data led to the creation of statistical analyzes. To 1918, the financial data in the US had been unsystematised and presented in the form of different measures. In 1918, the United States Senate issued a report[52] listing 31 500 companies whose profit was higher than 15%. The aim of this document was to estimate the profit reached in this period related to speculations connected with military actions. The results of this report were to present company efficiency and allow us for their future taxation. Other academics, such as J. E. Sterrett (1916) and R. Epstein[53] (1925) also studied company efficiency measurement in that period. The most extensive data on company results was presented in 1929 by L. Crum. It covered the period of 1916–1927 and included information from 455 000 companies. The main idea analysed in this study was the concept of a fair rate. The research conducted from the perspective of business and analytical practice could develop thanks to the contribution of an important person – L. H. Sloan[54], a forerunner of Standard and Poor's. This data significantly contributed to further research and studies related to measuring company performance. Based on the data, another important contribution to the development of studies from the scientific perspective was made by I. Fisher[55], publishing his book which in 1930 greatly affected the continuation of studies on company efficiency. In his monograph, he presented a theory of distribution, taking into account an individual's preference of present over future goods. This relation allowed for the emergence of a bonus, which is an interest rate informing how much an individual can pay to have goods available now and not in the future, which resulted from behaviors connected with the lack of patience or the desire to satisfy one's need. Further development of the scientific approach was possible thanks to J. Hirschleifer[56], who in 1958 presented a method of making optimal investment decisions while taking the Net

---

[52] *Corporate Earnings and Government Revenues.*

[53] R. C. Epstein. Industrial Profits in 1917. *The Quarterly Journal of Economics*, 39(2): 241–266.

[54] L. H. Sloan. 1929. *Corporate Profits, A Study of Their Size, Variation, Use and Distribution in a Period of Prosperity*. New York: Harper and Brothers Publishers.

[55] I. Fisher. *The Theory of Interest*. New York: The MacMillan Company.

[56] J. Hirschleifer. *On the Theory of Optimal Investment Decision. The Journal of Political Economy*, 66 (4). 329 –352.

Present Value[57] and Internal Rate of Return[58] into consideration. In 1962, M. J. Gordon[59] contributed to the research of his predecessors, conducting a study related to a dividend, and presented a model of dividend constant growth. At the end of the 1960s, in his monograph David Solomons[60] stressed the importance of the previous research, analysing fifty of the most significant companies in the US, and addressed the problems of achieved study results caused by the usage of booking data of not always the highest quality for calculating return rates.[61]

The efficiency of company operations, or the outcomes of the implemented strategy, can be measured with the use of financial and non-financial measures. In general, based on the secondary sources, three groups of financial measures can be distinguished[62]:

- Accounting ratios – used in the ratio analysis, based on data from previous periods, focusing on comparing revenues and costs in order to measure the rate of return on different levels of an income statement,
- Financial ratio – based on cash flows. This group of ratios excludes the imperfections of accounting ratios which result from used accounting principles or methods of pricing assets liabilities. Some ratios pertain to future situation and can usually be difficult to access by external parties. They involve a certain degree of uncertainty and, as a result, it is required to keep the company situation under the management supervision, in order to, if

---

57 NPV.

58 IRR

59 M. J. Gordon. *The Savings, Investment and Valuation of a Corporation, The Review of Economics and Statistics* 44:1. 37–51.

60 D. Solomons. 1965. *Divisional Performance: Measurement and Control, Financial Executives.* Nowy Jork.

61 W. N. Goetzman, and S. J. Garstka. 1999. *The Development of Corporate Performance Measures: Benchmarks before EVA$^{TM}$*, Yale ICF Working Paper 99-06, http://dx.doi.org/10.2139/ssrn.170674.

62 R. Wilczyński. *Pomiar efektywności a cele przedsiębiorstw,* Zeszyty Naukowe Uniwersytetu Szczecińskiego no. 803, "Finanse, Rynki Finansowe, Ubezpieczenia" no. 66, Szczecin: Wydawnictwo Naukowe Uniwersytetu Szczecińskiego: 1-12, www.wneiz.pl/frfu.

applicable, show deviations from values represented by these ratios,

- Market ratios – they are important for stockholders. They include both historic financial data, current situation, and planned future events in a company. In fact, they present the efficiency in the purchase of stocks more than the efficiency of company functioning.

Efficiency measurement can be extended and show not only financial, but also non-financial measures.

**Table 3. Methods of measuring financial performance (the historical approach)**

| **Measurement based on financial and accounting categories** | | **Measurement based on financial and accounting, as well as market and cash categories** | **Measurement based on financial and non-financial market and cash categories** | **Measurement based on non-financial categories** |
|---|---|---|---|---|
| 1920s | 1970s | 1980s | 1990s | 21st century |
| • DuPont Model – correlations between return on equity measures<br>• Return on Assets ratio (ROA)<br>• Return on Invested Capital (ROIC) | • Earnings per Share (EPS) | • Market Value Versus Book Value (MV/BV) or Tobin's Q ratio<br>• Return on Equity (ROE)<br>• Free Cash Flow (FCF) | • Economic earnings (Economic Value Added, EVA™<br>• Market Value Added (MVA)<br>• Cash Flow Return on Investment (CFROI) and Cash Value Added (CVA)<br>• Total shareholder return (TSR)<br>• Shareholder value added (SVA)<br>• Balanced scorecard (BSC) | • Value Creation Index (VCI)<br>• Measures of intellectual capital, e.g., Value Added Intellectual Coefficient — VAIC |

Source: G. Gołębiowski, and P. Szczepankowski. 2007. *Analiza wartości przedsiębiorstwa.* Warszawa: Difin: 18.

Over the years, with the growth of knowledge on companies, better access to data, and continuous scientific development, new trends and directions in the measurement of company performance have been determined (Table 3).

Some researchers identify efficiency with profitability, which is justified when based on a financial analysis. However, measuring company operations from the perspective of profitability also has its drawbacks:

- It includes booking measures that result from the accounting practices and thus, may be subject to manipulation,
- It refers to the past, so it focuses on a separated business activity, without considering how the surrounding affects a given company,
- It omits the issues related to risk, dividend policy, or cash value changes in time, which can be related to achieved return overrating,
- It does not take the company capital structure into consideration[63].

Non-financial measures were introduced in the 21st century and include such measures as:

- Value Creation Index[64] – it informs whether the return on equity is higher than the cost of equity, which is the case when this ratio is higher than 100%. In such a case, the generated value is higher than the company equity. Thus, the cost of equity is covered with the generated value, and the capital is generated which can be used in a company to cover, for instance, its operations or investments. VCI is calculated with the use of the following formula:

$$\frac{\text{ROE}}{\text{cost of equity}} x100\%$$

[63] M. Walczak (ed.). 2003. *Analiza finansowa w zarządzaniu przedsiębiorstwem*. Warszawa, p.
[64] VCI.

- Measures of intellectual capital (Value Added Intellectual Coefficient[65])[66] – a traditional approach in accounting was based on the cost approach, while this coefficient was to measure the efficiency from the perspective of using resources in a long-term time horizon. Value added in a company is created from the following resources:
- Employed capital – it includes physical and intellectual capital,
- Intellectual capital – it includes human and structural capital.

In general, the second group – financial measures of assessing company efficiency – includes three groups of measures[67]:

- Accounting measures Table 4),
- Financial measures (Table 5),
- Market measures (Table 6).

In addition to accounting measures, there are also financial measures (Table 5).

As an addition to accounting and financial measures, there are also market measures (Table 6).

It shall be emphasized that apart from financial ratios measuring company efficiency, there are also non-financial measures, used from as early as the mid-20th century by General Electric, which had listed the most important non-financial measures[68]:

- Market share,
- Productivity,

---

[65] VAIC™.

[66] J. Fijałkowska, Justyna. 2012. *VAIC™ jako metoda pomiaru dokonań przedsiębiorstw.* Zarządzanie i Finanse 11.1, part 2. Gdańsk: Uniwersytet Gdański: 68.

[67] A. Jaki. 2012. *Mechanizmy procesu zarządzania wartością przedsiębiorstwa.* Kraków: UE: 152.

[68] D. Otley, *Measuring Performance: The Accounting Perspective*, [w:] A. Neely (red.), *Business Performance Measurement. Theory and practice*, Cambridge University Press, Cambridge 2006, s. 17.

## Table 4. Accounting measures of company efficiency

| ACCOUNTING MEASURES OF EFFICIENCY | | |
|---|---|---|
| **Absolute measures** | | |
| EBIT | NP + INT + T | EBIT – Earnings Before Interest (Operating Profit) |
| | | NP – Net Profit |
| | | INT – Interest |
| | | T – Tax |
| EBITDA | EBIT + DEP | EBITDA – Earnings Before Interest, Taxes, Depreciation, and Amortization |
| | | EBIT – Earnings Before Interest (Operating Profit) |
| | | DEP – Depreciation |
| NOPAT | EBIT x (1 - T) | NOPAT – Net Operating Profit After Tax |
| | | EBIT – Earnings Before Interest (Operating Profit) |
| | | T – tax |
| EBIDAAT | (EBIT + DEP) x (1 - T) | EBIDAAT – Earnings Before Interest, Depreciation and Amortization, After Taxes |
| | | EBIT – Earnings Before Interest (Operating Profit) |
| | | DEP – Depreciation |
| | | T – Tax |
| EPS | NP/number of shares | EPS – Earnings per Share |
| ROI | NOPAT/K | ROI – Return on Invested Capital |
| | | NOPAT – Net Operating Profit After Tax |
| | | K – total capital |
| ROA | NP/A | ROA – net Return on Assets |
| | | NP – Net Profit |
| | | A – total assets |
| ROS | NP/S | ROS – Return on Sales |
| | | NP – Net Profit |
| | | S – net sales |
| **Relative measures** | | |
| ROE | NP/E | NP – Net Profit |
| | | E – Equity |
| DFL | (ROE - ROI)/ROI | DFL – Degree of Financial Leverage |
| | | ROE – Return on Equity |
| | | ROI – Return on Invested Capital |
| DOL | (S - VC)/EBIT | DOL – Degree of Operational Leverage |
| | | S – net sales |
| | | VC – Variable Costs |

Source: A. Jaki. 2008. Zarządzanie wartością – pomiar i ocena kreowania wartości. *Świat Nieruchomości* no. 64, 10-15.

- Product leadership,
- Personnel development,
- Employee attitudes,
- Public responsibility.

B. Nita[69] presents measures divided into more and less important ones. Important measures in the following countries include:

1. The Great Britain:
    - Percentage share of deliveries as per schedule,
    - The number of complaints,
    - The number of returns,
    - Productivity,
    - Efficiency,
    - Defects,
2. Italy
    - Productivity,
    - Waste,
    - Percentage share of deliveries as per schedule,
    - The number of defects,
    - The number of complaints,
3. Japan
    - The number of complaints,
    - The number of defects,
    - Waste,
    - Percentage share of deliveries as per schedule,
    - The use of potential,
4. Canada
    - Percentage share of deliveries as per schedule,
    - The number of complaints,
    - Productivity in manufacturing,

---

[69] B. Nita. 2014. *Niefinansowy pomiar dokonań przedsiębiorstw produkcyjnych w teorii i praktyce*. Prace Naukowe, UE Wrocław nr 335, Wrocław: 191.

- Activity level,
- The number of defects.

### Table 5. Financial measures of company efficiency

| FINANCIAL MEASURES OF EFFICIENCY | | |
|---|---|---|
| **Absolute measures** | | |
| FCF | NOPAT + DEP - I - ΔWC | FCF – Free Cash Flow |
| | | NOPAT – Net Operating Profit After Tax |
| | | DEP – Depreciation |
| | | I – investment capital |
| | | ΔWC – net change in working capital |
| FCFE | NP + DEP - I -ΔWC + ΔD | FCFE – Free Cash Flow to Equity |
| | | NP – Net Profit |
| | | DEP – Depreciation |
| | | I – investment capital |
| | | ΔWC – net change in working capital |
| | | ΔD – net increase in debt |
| GCF | NOPAT + DEP | GCF – Gross Cash Flow |
| | | NOPAT – Net Operating Profit After Tax |
| | | DEP – Depreciation |
| DCF | $CF \times 1/(1 + r)^n$ | DCF – Discounted Cash Flow |
| | | CF – Cash Flow |
| | | r – discount rate |
| | | n – number of years |
| NPV | $\sum NCF \times 1/(1 + r)^n - \sum I\ 1/(1 + r)^n$ | NPV – Net Present Value |
| | | NCF – Net Cash Flow |
| | | r – discount rate |
| | | n – number of years |
| | | I – investment capital |
| CVA | K x (CFROI - WACC) = GCF - K x WACC | CVA – Cash Value Added |
| | | K – total capital |
| | | CFROI – Cash Flow Return on Investment |
| | | WACC – Weighted Average Cost of Capital |
| | | GCF – Gross Cash Flow |
| IRR | $\sum NCF \times 1/(1 + IRR)^n = \sum I \times 1/(1 + IRR)^n$ | IRR – Internal Return Rate |
| | | NCF – Net Cash Flow |
| | | n – number of years |

| Relative measures | | |
|---|---|---|
| CFROI | $\sum NCF \times 1/(1 + CFROI)^n = \sum I \times 1/(1 + CFROI)^n$ | CFROI – Cash Flow Return on Investment |
| | | NCF – Net Cash Flow |
| | | n – number of years |
| WACC | $k_e \times E/K + k_d \times D/K$ | WACC – Weighted Average Cost of Capital |
| | | ke – cost of equity |
| | | kd – cost of foreign capital (debt) |
| | | E – equity |
| | | D – foreign capital (debt) |
| | | K – total capital |

Source: A. Jaki. 2008. Zarządzanie wartością – pomiar i ocena kreowania wartości. *Świat Nieruchomości* no. 64, 10-15.

## Table 6. Market measures of company efficiency

| MARKET MEASURES OF EFFICIENCY | | |
|---|---|---|
| **Absolute measures** | | |
| EVA$^{TM}$ | K x (ROI - WACC) = NOPAT - K x WACC | EVA$^{TM}$ – Economic Value Added |
| | | K – total capital |
| | | ROI – Return on Invested capital |
| | | WACC – Weighted Average Cost of Capital |
| | | NOPAT – Net Operating Profit After Tax |
| EVC | $E \times (ROE - k_e) = NP - E \times k_e$ | EVC – Estimated Value Created |
| | | ROE – Return on Equity |
| | | ke – cost of equity |
| | | NP – Net Profit |
| MVA | V(K) - K = V(E) - E | MVA – Market Value Added |
| | | V(K) – market value of capital |
| | | V(E) – market value of equity |
| | | K – total capital |
| | | E – equity |
| SVA | $\Delta V(E) = DIV - I$ | SVA – Shareholder Value Added |
| | | $\Delta V(E)$ – increase of market value of equity |
| | | DIV – dividends paid during the year |
| | | I – net investments of stockholders |
| **Relative measures** | | |
| TSR | $[(P_1 - P_0) + DPS]/P_0$ | TSR – total shareholder return (return on shares) |
| | | $P_1P_0$ – market price of shares as of the beginning and end of the period |
| | | DPS – dividend per share paid in a given period |

Source: A. Jaki. 2008. Zarządzanie wartością – pomiar i ocena kreowania wartości. *Świat Nieruchomości* no. 64, 10-15.

Factors which are less important include:

- Precision in estimating batches,
- Staff rotation,
- Late employees,
- Hours worked overtime,
- Employee satisfaction results.

Thus, financial factors are important in measuring company efficiency, but they can be complemented with non-financial factors.

## 1.5. Efficient Functioning of Companies in the Context of Globalization

In the 21st century, globalization process in almost all areas of life definitely accelerated and developed. Globalization as it is currently known was shaped by the following stages[70]:

- The Age of Trade (1500–1850) – it was a period of travelling and trade. Goods were carried from different, often remote and exotic countries in order to profit from selling them in Europe.
- 1850–1914, when business was based on supporting state companies. Less developed or politically dependent countries functioned as a back-up supply of resources.
- The Age of Concession (1914–1945) – the times when the state protectionism dominated. Less developed countries used privileges and other inducements to attract foreign investors, with economic benefits of increased employment and social advantages such as social care.

[70] P. Maśloch. 2011. *Restrukturyzacja przedsiębiorstw w Polsce w dobie transformacji i globalizacji*. Toruń: WSB Toruń: 32.

- The National Age (1945–1970) – a period of dissolving colonies and developing the market which encouraged investment. Conducted actions were related to the economic expansion of the United States and Japan, the latter of which became an economic power and world economy business leader.
- The Global Age (since 1970) – companies stopped operating only on local or national markets and expanded to continental and global ones. This allowed for a faster increase in sales, leading to the growth of an accumulated margin, which resulted in a higher net profit and a possible increase of a company value.

They are connected with technological progress and greater mutual relations of different economies. Economic processes are related to operations of two entities, such as companies and households. Management is based on the following chain: production – division – exchange – consumption. Currently, the management process is not determined by country borders, but by the reach of different types of capital connections. The following areas of globalization can be distinguished:

- Globalization of finances – global capital mobility, possible fast cash flow in the world, political borders of the countries are left aside, there is greater risk of an economic bubble due to the inflow of a significant part of the world capital to the country where financial instruments of different risk level are used, including hybrid instruments[71], which creates the possibility to reach outstanding return rates,
- Globalization of markets and competition – international cooperation between companies, a possibility to dynamically

[71] More about hybrid instruments: J. Węcławski. 2006. *Hybrydowe instrumenty finansowania przedsiębiorstw*. [In:] *Finanse przedsiębiorstwa*, P. Karpuś (ed.). Lublin: UMCS: 139–147, J. Węcławski. 1997. *Venture Capital. Nowy instrument finansowania przedsiębiorstw*. Warszawa: PWN: 17.

transfer from being a company which operates on a country level or dominates on a given continent, to being a global enterprise,
- Globalization of technology and knowledge – improved information flow; technological development in the world creates better circumstances to take innovative actions,
- Globalization of consumption and lifestyle – globalization can lead to the loss of individualism or reduce cultural separateness in countries; there is a desire to strive for unification and standardization of behavior. Such actions can foster the development of mergers and acquisitions, the increase of sales at a global scale, increased standardization of products which is visible in the sale of the same product in the whole world, easier contact with the consumers thanks to the development of mass media. Such actions can lead to the concentration of capital available in the world, better brand recognizability and, as a result, to the increase in value of companies, which can grow bigger in their reach than the territory of some countries,
- Globalization of legal regulations – it leads to greater political unification and facilitates acquisition processes, capital flow, and decisions about entering new markets; it also allows for easier movement of persons. One of the examples of such actions was the harmonization of legal regulations in the European Union countries, which had to adjust their laws to EU's requirements and regulations.[72]

Globalization is a multidimensional process with the following characteristics:

- Different factors simultaneously affecting company operations,
- Consolidation of operations conducted by entities with a global reach,
- Interdependence of entities and economies,

[72] R. Borowiecki, E. Wysłocka. 2012. *Analiza ekonomiczna i ocena ekspercka w procesie restrukturyzacji przedsiębiorstw*. Warszawa: Difin: 18.

- Strict relations with technological progress,
- Blurring barriers of cooperation in the form of territorial distance; compression of time and space,
- Positive influence on company development. However, there are also actions of a completely opposite nature and negative character,
- Global economy as the biggest unit and a point of reference. Development is not yet possible at this stage.[73]

Due to internationalization, companies need to create strategies adjusted to the needs of the global market. Strategy execution is based on achieving objectives specified in the form of directions of changes and adaptation methods (Figure 6). These elements emphasize the complexity of the globalization process.

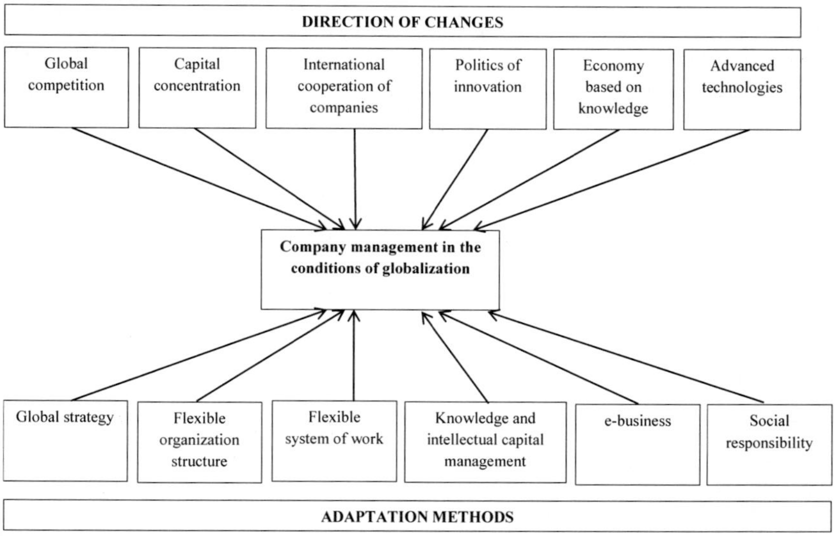


Source: R. Borowiecki, E. Wysłocka. 2012. *Analiza ekonomiczna i ocena ekspercka w procesie restrukturyzacji przedsiębiorstw*. Warszawa: Difin: 21.

Figure 6. Companies in the context of globalization.

[73] M. Malinowska, B. Kucharska, ed. 2006. *Zachowania podmiotów rynkowych w warunkach globalizacji*. Warszawa: PWE: 16.

Employee experience and knowledge are important factors for a company, as they affect the company competitive advantage, which, in turn, can lead to increased company value. Human resources management accelerates and improves processes in a company and, in some cases, streamlines or even eliminates processes which make entity operations longer.[74]

The increase of significance of knowledge and intellectual property led to the introduction of a term "new economy", which is related to such elements as the development of technology and innovation or global competition. The learning process takes place faster and affects employees' work, ensuring greater performance. This, in turn, affects company's efficiency, position among the competitors, and, as a result, economic growth. Due to frequently performed innovative actions, many fixed assets become outdated or obsolete. The way a company is perceived changes, as well as the way vision, mission, or strategy is determined. The development of global companies leads to the introduction of new forms of business management based on achieved effects, evaluated with the use of measures and coefficients. Control measures result in the execution of operations and strategy introduced by the owners. Approach to control and supervision over operations (and also over the achievement of set company objectives) in spread units operating in the whole world is based on proper tools and instruments needed to maintain and channel reliable information with the use of documents (financial statements), but not only. These documents show a historic company situation after accounting settlement, so after a specific time. Greater territorial reach requires more time in order to allow for the preparation of documents, for instance, financial statements. Company operations must be regularly supervised, therefore KPIs[75] are used to inform about the current company situation[76].

KPIs allow us to check the level of achieved strategic objectives. KPIs in a given company include financial and non-financial indicators which reveal problems at their initial stage and allow us to react by improving

[74] Ibidem: 22.
[75] Key Performance Indicators.
[76] F. Krawiec. 2005. *Transformacja firmy w nowej gospodarce. Koncepcje, strategie, struktury, struktury i technologie w zarządzaniu*. Difin: 158.

processes. In order to be useful and inform about the company situation at an early stage, KPIs must have the following characteristics:

- Indicators must be related to the elements in the strategy,
- Indicators must be adjusted to the specific character of the company business activity and industry,
- There should be an optimum, and not too high number of indicators informing about the most important processes and events in a company. KPI is not supposed to inform about all processes, only about the most important ones,
- Indicators should have a point of reference in the form of data from previous periods or industry data,
- A company should focus on indicators which can be controlled by the management and employees,
- To a large extent, indicators can be based on customers' satisfaction and content level,
- The costs of informing/calculating indicators cannot be higher than the benefits from using them,
- Indicators should be easy to understand for employees and accessible to them on a regular basis, in order to allow for the creation of analyzes for previous periods, leading to conclusions and setting new objectives to achieve.[77]

The elements which affect the development of globalization and of companies can be categorized into the following categories[78]:

- Competition
  - Economic cooperation,
  - Significant dynamics in the growth of developing countries,

[77] M. Rydzewska-Włodarczyk, M. Sobieraj. 2015. *Pomiar efektywności procesów za pomocą kluczowych wskaźników efektywności*, Zeszyty Naukowe Uniwersytetu Szczecińskiego no. 864, Finanse, Rynki Finansowe, Ubezpieczenia no. 76 v. 2, Szczecin: 339.

[78] T. Brake, D. Walker. 1995. *Doing business internationally. The workbook to cross – cultural success*. Princeton: Training Management Corporation: 4.

  - Greater competitive advantage
- Technology
  - Production and distribution tailored to needs,
  - New technologies influencing the development of information transfer methods and effective communication,
- Markets
  - The existence of brands of a global reach,
- Government
  - Elimination of trade barriers,
  - Adjustment to new technologies and innovation,
- Customers
  - Greater importance of product quality,
  - Providing post-sale services.

Conducting business activity in changeable conditions and on international level can be directed with a proper strategy (Figure 7)[79]:

- International strategy – its advantage is the usage of know-how acquired on different markets. Possible difficulties can include the need to adapt one's offer to specific regions, or the difficulty of effective usage of a company geographical reach of operations,
- Global strategy – business development related to the optimization of territorial reach of a business activity. Adapting the offer to local environment can be a challenge,
- Multinational strategy – a possibility to adapt at a regional level, no possibility to optimize the reach of business activity resulting from territorial limitation to a level of several countries, and not a global one,
- Transnational strategy – a possibility to adapt one's offer to a regional level and expand, resulting from conducting a business activity globally. Possible discrepancies resulting from the objectives of an applied strategy can be a challenge.

---

[79] J. Lichtarski. 2001. *Podstawy nauki o przedsiębiorstwie*. Wrocław: AE: 404.

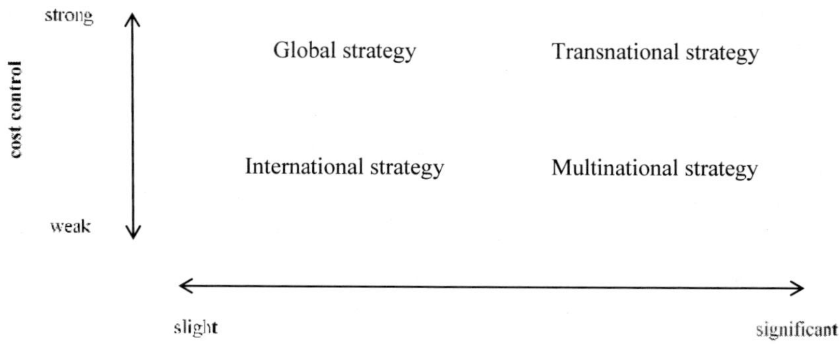


Source: J. Lichtarski. 2001. *Podstawy nauki o przedsiębiorstwie*. Wrocław: AE: 400.

Figure 7. Types of strategies applied by international companies.

Focusing on globalization, we can distinguish its main categories[80]:

- Globalization of finances and capital ownership – aiming at the transactions of mergers and acquisitions, possible international transfer of capital in a short time,
- Globalization of markets and strategies – starting business cooperation, searching for development possibilities outside of one's country,
- Globalization of technology, research, and knowledge – the development of technology is an important factor, which allows to grow a global network of connections,
- Globalization of lifestyle – it is connected with a standardization of lifestyle in the world. A growing group of people lives and behaves according to standards imposed by mass media, which leads to the increase of brand recognizability and company net profit, but also to the loss of local identity, culture, and tradition. What is more, the global reach of one's business activity makes even bigger entry barriers for the companies than before,
- Globalization of legal regulations – actions aiming at creating conglomerates of countries and legal norms that apply on the

[80] Grupa Lizbońska. 1996. *Granice konkurencji*. Warszawa: Poltext: 49.

international level (for example such creations of the European Union),

- Globalization as a political standardization – the acceptance of political and economic cooperation by most societies. Creating a uniform global system of merging processes and increasing the integration of societies and their connecting systems,
- Globalization of awareness – losing the attachment to nationality, culture, and religion and aiming at reaching the perspective of "a citizen of the world".

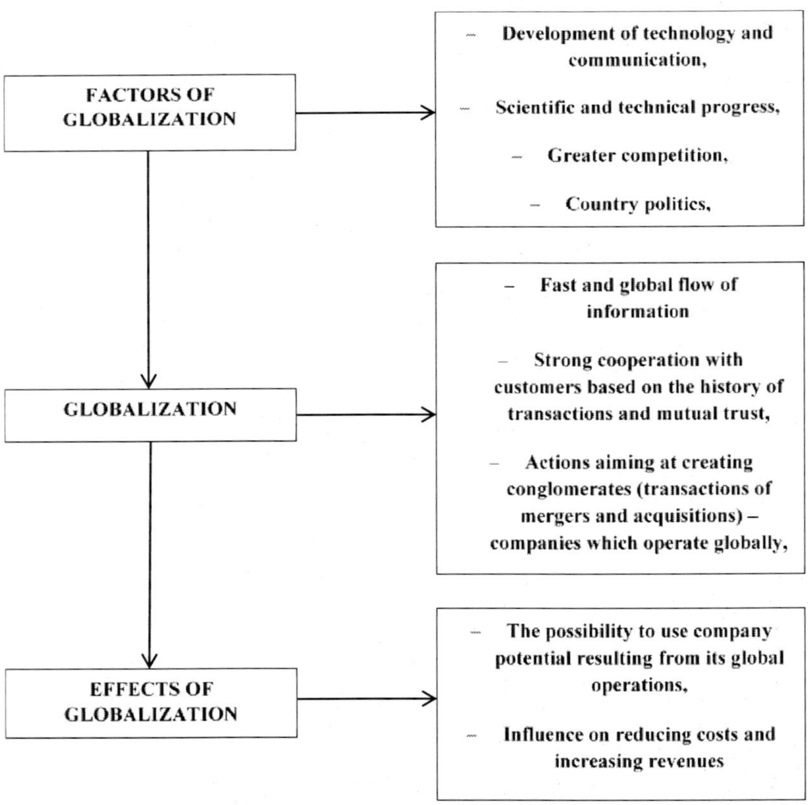


Source: P. Maśloch. 2011. *Restrukturyzacja przedsiębiorstw w Polsce w dobie transformacji i globalizacji.* Toruń 2011: WSB: 73.

Figure 8. The course of globalization process and its effect on companies.

The process of globalization can be divided into three stages (Figure 8):

- Stage 1 – factors of globalization,
- Stage 2 – globalization,
- Stage 3 – effects of globalization.

*Chapter 2*

# RESTRUCTURING COMPANIES

## 2.1. DEFINING APPROACH

Restructuring is an extreme choice of company owners or managers, aiming at restoring an internal balance in a company, as well as at improving completely or partially lost relations of their company with its environment[81].

When dealing with a difficult situation of a company, it is important to strive at restructuring such a company and avoid its bankruptcy, which, in general, is related to two types of costs, including directs costs of bankruptcy, such as the costs of bankruptcy proceedings, bankruptcy estate employees, and indirect ones in the form of lost chances of sale or hindered access to financing. Expected costs of bankruptcy can be calculated with the use of a formula including: the likeability of bankruptcy multiplied by the cost of bankruptcy expressed in a percentage share of the company market value. However, the companies which are under the biggest threat of a significant deterioration of their situation in times of crisis are those which use leveraging to a large extent[82].

---

[81] Z. Sapijaszka. 1997. *Restrukturyzacja przedsiębiorstwa. Szanse i ograniczenia*. Warszawa: PWN: 23.

[82] C. Krishnamurti, S.R. Vishwanath. 2008. *Mergers, Acquisitions and Corporate Restructuring*. London: Business Books from SAGE: 338–340.

## Table 7. Definitions of restructuring in Polish and foreign sources

| Author | Definition |
|---|---|
| A. Kamela-Sowińska, A. B. Mirecki | Restructuring is a process of organizational, economic, financial, and technical adaptation of a company which is the most suitable for the company objective. It is also a set of actions aiming at increasing efficiency and using resources in conducted business activity in order to ensure competitive advantage in the market. |
| R. Borowiecki | Restructuring is a systemic transformation, modernization, or advancement of company organizational structure and the principles of business functioning and other objects of economic research. |
| H. Jagoda, J. Lichtarski | Restructuring of a company – a complex set of terms which describe all types of structural changes in a company. It can apply to the structure of property, capital, organization, management, employment, production and product offer, supply and sale market, technical and technological one, etc. From this perspective, restructuring seems to function as an equivalent of a term of "reorganization" which is widely used in reference to strictly understood organizational changes. |
| Z. Jasiński | Restructuring is a reorientation of company objectives, thought-out in the context of changes in the company environment, and the adaptation of technology, organization, economics, and human resources to such objectives. |
| I. Duplik | Restructuring is usually defined as a systemic transformation, modernization, advancement, or the adaptation of a company, firm, or institution structure to the current level of technology and organization-management thought.<br>However, in the context of Poland, restructuring is associated with privatization and macroeconomic changes. |
| A. Nalepka | Company restructuring is a thought-out reorientation of company objectives (mission) suitably to changes that have or are to take place in the environment, and a relevant adaptation of technology, organization, economics, and human resources. |
| B. Pełka | Company restructuring means systemic changes in company technology, production organization, management system, economics, and market, as well as in company organizational and legal status. |
| A. Stabryła | Restructuring is a diagnostic and project-related process aiming at improving the management and exploitation system and the use of human resources. |
| J. Penc | Restructuring is a complex and comprehensive transformation of a business activity with regard to its material and non-material, operational and strategic activity area. Restructuring includes necessary systemic adaptive actions subject to the efficiency criterion and the objective of company operations strategy. |

| Author | Definition |
|---|---|
| D. Kowalczuk-Jakubowska, A. Malewicz | Restructuring is a process the essence of which is the diversification of actions and modernization of production structure in a company, implementing new production techniques and technologies, quality improvement, sale activization, etc. Restructuring aims at reaching a better strategic position of a company on the market and, as a result, at achieving better results. |
| H. Singh | Restructuring is a drastic change in company assets, capital structure, or organizational structure. |
| M. Blatz, S. Haghani | Restructuring is an intended process oriented to ensuring that a company survives in a short time, and to restoring its competitive advantage in the market. |
| R. Myers | Restructuring is a strategic process aiming at the maximization of economy value and its subjects. |
| J. L. Bicksler, A. H. Chen | Restructuring is a strategy of growth and economy reorientation (of a sector, region, or business entity). |

Source: M. Mozalewski. 2010. Rodzaje i metody restrukturyzacji przedsiębiorstw, Ruch Prawniczy, *Ekonomiczny i Socjologiczny*, no. 2. Poznań: UE Poznań: 216. R. Borowiecki. 2014. *Zarządzanie restrukturyzacją przedsiębiorstw i gospodarki.* Kraków: Fundacja UE Kraków: 14–18.

Fundamental changes in a company often result from the influence of changes in the company environment. In secondary literature, we can find many definitions of restructuring, depending on the type of restructuring and used tools (Table 7).

Restructuring is required in the processes of adapting to changes in the company business environment.[83] These changes can be of following nature[84]:

- Adaptive – adaptation to environment changes is postponed and takes place after the changes in the business environment,
- Innovative – the introduction of changes which are to precede changes in a business environment.

[83] R. Borowiecki, A. Nalepka. 2003. *Restrukturyzacja w procesie funkcjonowania i rozwoju przedsiębiorstw*. [In:] R. Borowiecki (ed.). 2003. *Zarządzanie restrukturyzacją procesów gospodarczych. Aspekt teoretyczno – praktyczny*. Warszawa: Difin: 76.

[84] Z. Sapijaszka. 1997. *Restrukturyzacja przedsiębiorstwa. Szanse i ograniczenia*. Warszawa: PWN: 16.

In fact, the introduction of changes is related to the implementation of innovative solutions, but it does not have to work the other way around, as not every change is an innovation. The following stages of changes are distinguished[85]:

- Stage 1 – the awareness of changes – a decision about implementing changes is taken after the analysis of the company situation. Monitoring the current state of the company leads to drawing certain conclusions and taking further steps. Introduction of changes results thus from insufficient efficiency of company functioning and is related to the unused company potential.
- Stage 2 – identification of changes – it is crucial to come to certain conclusions based on stage 1, and to recognize what changes need to be introduced in order to improve the company functioning.
- Stage 3 – implementation of changes – after a precise recognition of changes, there is an implementation stage. It is important to set a schedule of implementing changes and to monitor effects. Planned achievements should be verified against the actual ones, and it is necessary to find the reasons for any deviations between these two.
- Stage 4 – integration of changes – if the introduced changes have affected the internal and external situation of the company, the introduced changes should be subject to standardization in order to have them fit company executed strategy and organizational culture.

There are different classifications of restructuring, depending on the accepted criterion. Restructuring can be divided into levels[86]:

---

[85] S. R. Hernandez, A. D. Kaluzny. 2000. *Innowacje i zmiany organizacyjne.* [In:] S. M. Shortell, A. D. Kaluzny. *Podstawy zarządzania opieką zdrowotną*. Kraków: Versalius: 378.

[86] Z. Malara. 2001. *Restrukturyzacja organizacyjna przedsiębiorstwa.* Wrocław: Oficyna Wydawnicza Politechniki Wrocławskiej: 16.

1. Level 1 – the character of changes
   - Rehabilitation restructuring
   - Development restructuring:
   
     – Creative restructuring,
     
     – Anticipation restructuring
     
     – Adjustment restructuring
2. Level 2 – the form of restructuring
   - Subject-based restructuring
   - Object-based restructuring
3. Level 3 – the area of restructuring
   - Operating restructuring
   - Restructuring of a scope of activity
   - Financial restructuring
   - Organizational restructuring

Referring the definitions of restructuring and its stages, one should also focus on the reasons for restructuring, which can depend on the following factors:

1. Internal factors[87]:
   - Poor management,
   - Improper financial control,
   - Unstable and high cost level,
   - Insufficient marketing actions,
   - The scope of activity which outstrips financial possibilities,
   - Chaos in the organization,
   - Improper financial policy.

---

[87] S. Slatter, D. Lovett. 2001. *Restrukturyzacja firmy. Zarządzanie przedsiębiorstwem w sytuacjach kryzysowych*. Warszawa: WIG-Press: 17.

2. External factors[88]:
    - Changes in the demand for products and services,
    - Competitors' impact,
    - Incorrect pricing policy.

Other reasons can also include the process of adapting a company to its environment, which can be divided into[89]:

1. Functional changes:
    - Removing internal disturbances,
    - Overcoming a disadvantageous situation in the environment.
2. Structural changes:
    - Removing internal disturbances,
    - Overcoming a disadvantageous situation in the environment.

Basic aims of company restructuring mostly include[90]:

1. Controlling and eliminating direct symptoms of a crisis – stabilization of the company situation and an attempt to resolve or ease the crisis,
2. Restoring the interest group support – proper cooperation with suppliers and recipients,
3. Ensuring future sources of financing – financial restructuring,
4. Company reorganization – the change in the organization of operations and process improvement.

---

[88] Ibidem: 36.

[89] P. Maśloch. 2011. *Restrukturyzacja przedsiębiorstw w Polsce w dobie transformacji i globalizacji*. Toruń: WSB: 84.

[90] C. Suszyński. 2003. *Restrukturyzacja, konsolidacja, globalizacja przedsiębiorstw. Doświadczenia i perspektywy polskiej transformacji*. Warszawa: PWE: 124.

## 2.2. Types of Company Restructuring

There are numerous classifications of restructuring tools and methods. Restructuring can be conducted with the following approaches applied:[91]

1. Asset restructuring
   - Sale of a part of company assets (*asset sales*),
     - Sale of a subsidy or the production line (*spin-off, split off, split up*),
     - Sale of subsidy stocks (*equity carve-out),*
     - Company sell-off (*sell-off, divestitures*)
   - Sale of all company assets for cash which is paid to stockholders (*liquidation*)
2. Change in the ownership structure
   - Company share repurchases,
     - Market transactions (*open-market purchase*),
     - Tender procedure (*tender offer*),
     - Negotiations with stockholders (*private negotiation*)
   - Offering owned securities in exchange for others (*exchange offer*)
   - Privatization (*going-private transactions*)
     - Buyout transaction (*pure going-private transaction*)
     - Leveraged buyout *(LBO*)[92]
     - Management buyout *(MBO*)

From a different perspective, the following types of restructuring can be distinguished, depending on the applied criterion[93]:

1. The criterion of restructuring objectives:

---

[91] C. Suszyński. 2003. *Restrukturyzacja, konsolidacja, globalizacja przedsiębiorstw. Doświadczenia i perspektywy polskiej transformacji*. Warszawa: PWE: 142-143.

[92] More about leveraged buyouts can be found in: Z. Kuryłek. 2017. *Wykup lewarowany. Sposób akwizycji firm.* Warszawa: Difin.

[93] Z. Pierścionek. 1996. *Restrukturyzacja, a rozwój i strategie przedsiębiorstw.* [In:] *Restrukturyzacja w procesie przekształceń i rozwoju przedsiębiorstw*. TNOiK: AE Kraków: 170.

- Cost reduction,
- Maintaining competitive advantage.

2. The criterion of the scope and rate of changes:
   - Ground-breaking restructuring,
   - Incremental restructuring,
   - Permanent restructuring,
   - Restructuring conducted once in a given period.
3. The criterion of reach
   - Partial restructuring,
   - Complex restructuring,
   - Coordinated restructuring,
   - Uncoordinated restructuring,
4. The criterion of company systems:
   - Restructuring of production systems,
   - Restructuring of supply systems,
   - Restructuring of the management system,
   - Restructuring of the information system
5. The criterion of production factors types:
   - Restructuring of employment,
   - Fixed assets restructuring,
   - Subject of work restructuring.
6. The criterion of strategic resources:
   - Financial restructuring,
   - Fixed assets restructuring,
   - Restructuring of skills and labor resources.

There are many different types of restructuring which can be ordered in accordance to different criteria (Table 8).

There are numerous classifications of restructuring, and one more, apart from the above presented ones was proposed by C. Suszyński (Figure 9), included the division into subject- and object-based restructuring.

### Table 8. Restructuring criteria

| The criterion of a systemic transformation stage | The criterion of a territorial reach | The criterion of an area under restructuring | The criterion of process dynamics |
|---|---|---|---|
| Rehabilitation restructuring – used at the initial stage of rehabilitation actions. It is supposed to prevent accumulating negative financial results and, primarily, the loss of financial liquidity. This type of restructuring is connected to the reduction of property and employment. Taken actions are intended to prevent company bankruptcy and ineffective operations. | Macrorestructuring – it involves changing the whole structure of a given industry sector. It is connected with the change of proportion in the creation and division of the national income. | Object-related restructuring – the increase of company efficiency by reorganizing company organization, legal regulations, and economic sphere. This type of restructuring should result in the increase of company value with the use of significant changes (e.g., creating flexible structures in a company, such as departments of finances, controlling, accounting, logistics, marketing, sales, or by purchasing property, privatization, creating capital groups). | Traditional restructuring – it involves an effective use and development of available technical and economic resources. This type of restructuring is of an evolutionary nature and involves development by recognizing current processes and aiming at the best usage of all resources owned by a company. |
| Recuperation restructuring – it involves increasing company competitive advantage and maintaining it on the national market. Competitors serve as a point of reference; in order to catch up with them, a company needs to use its potential related to operations and human resources. | Mesorestructuring – streamlining processes in the whole sectors of industry or in the functioning of company conglomerates. | Subject-related restructuring – it involves technical and technological changes in a company. It may also refer to the production process by adapting production effectively to orders, creating new products without neglecting the development of currently the most popular products, as well as by introducing technical and product-related innovations. | Radical restructuring – it involves complete restructuring of operations and aiming at reaching the maximum client satisfaction and, at the same time, achieving satisfying financial results. |

**Table 8. (Continued)**

| The criterion of a systemic transformation stage | The criterion of a territorial reach | The criterion of an area under restructuring | The criterion of process dynamics |
|---|---|---|---|
| Development restructuring – aiming at maintaining and increasing the efficiency of operations by strengthening the company position on the market and striving for expansion into foreign markets. | Microrestructuring – involves changes in a company aiming at streamlining its functioning mostly by innovation in the context of products and services. | | |

Source: Z. Pastuszak. 1999. Restrukturyzacyjne skutki prywatyzacji przedsiębiorstw państwowych. *Technika, produkcja, logistyka*. Lubli: Politechnika Lubelska: 71, and A. Bitkowska. 2010. Przebieg procesu restrukturyzacji przedsiębiorstwa. [In:] Bitkowska A. (ed.) *Procesy restrukturyzacji warunkiem poprawy konkurencyjności przedsiębiorstw*. Warszawa: Difin: 48–56.

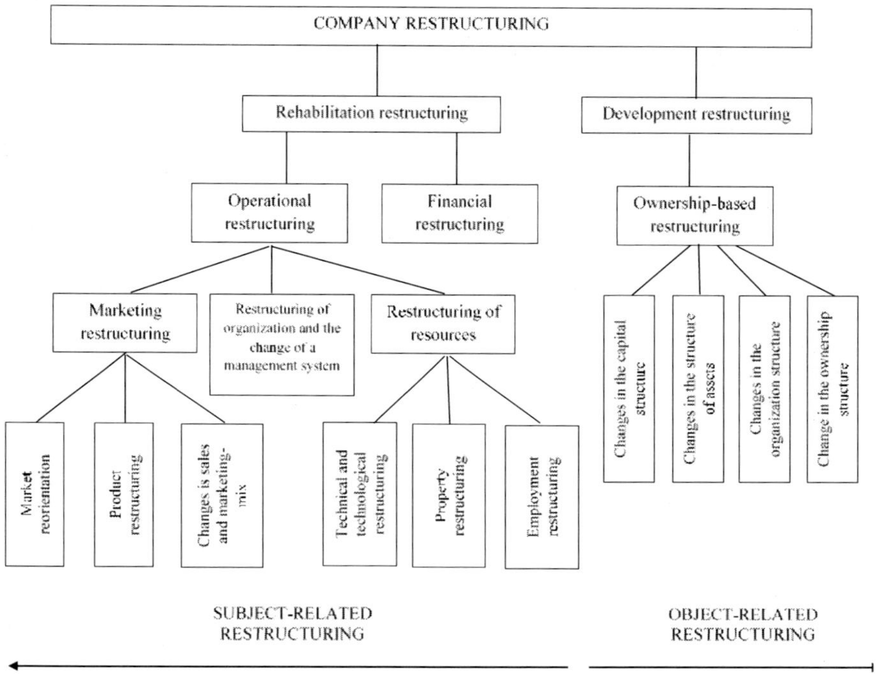


Source: C. Suszyński. 2009. *Restrukturyzacja przedsiębiorstw.* Warszawa: PWE: 184.

Figure 9. Types of company restructuring.

## 2.3. Tools for Company Restructuring

The main tools of company restructuring include the following elements:

### 2.3.1. Benchmarking

A method including a comparison with other companies and, based on that, evaluation whether adaptation processes should be introduced to increase company efficiency by implementing changes in the way operations are carried out. There are numerous definitions of benchmarking (Table 9), and its essence is related with finding other companies operating in the same industry in order to find a point of reference for one's own business activity.[94] Benchmarking has been used since the 1950s by companies in Japan. Their aim was to catch up in their development to the companies from Western European countries and the United States. The adaptation process can take place not only from the companies in the same industry, but also based on the best solutions in other industries. These solutions can include, e.g., the approach to production, quality management, the usage of IT or technical solutions, the method of implementing strategies.

Benchmarking consists of the following stages[95]:

- Identification – determining factors thanks to which a company is the best in its industry,
- Knowledge – evaluating the business activity of other companies while looking for things to change in the functioning of a given organization. It is a process of learning and using others' experience, as well as an attempt to understand business functioning of other companies,
- Adaptation – implementing changes resulting from the knowledge acquired,
- Systematization – collected information should be merged in a proper way to constitute a unified whole,
- Continuity – improving company functioning is a continuous process aiming at reaching perfection.

---

[94] B. Karlof, S. Stblom. 1995. *Benchmarking – równaj do najlepszych*. Warszawa: Biblioteka Menedżera i Bankowca: 35.

[95] T. Luque-Martınez Munoz, F. Leiva. 2005. *City Benchmarking: A Methodological Proposal Referring Specifically to Granada*. "Cities", Vol. 22, No. 6, 411-423.

**Table 9. Definitions of benchmarking in Polish and foreign literature**

| Author | Definition |
|---|---|
| W. M. Grudzewski, J. K. Hejduk | Benchmarking means comparing one's company with other organizations with better results or setting directions for development and adapting them to good ideas in order to improve. |
| J. Brilman | Benchmarking is a process of improving efficiency of one's organization by identifying, analyzing, adapting, and implementing ideas used by the most globally efficient organizations. |
| R. Camp | Benchmarking means searching for the most effective methods allowing to achieve competitive advantage of a given organization. |
| H. J. Harrington | An act of systematically determining the best systems, processes, procedures, and actions, which become models for the analysed organization |
| J. Czekaj | A method of searching for model ways of acting that allow you to achieve the best results by learning from others |
| J. Bank | A permanent element of company management process involving its comparison to the competitors, an element allowing you to evaluate a company and use thus acquired knowledge to prepare a practical plan of dominating the market |
| Węgrzyn | A continuous and systematic process of identifying, analyzing, preparing, and, as a result, implementing the best solutions regarding the processes of recognized and proven models in organizations, resulting in the increase of efficiency |
| American Productivity and Quality Center (APQC) | A systematic and continuous process of measuring and comparing business activity of a given organization to leaders of economic processes, aiming at finding information which will help this organization take actions to improve its functioning |
| Z. Martyniak | Learning from the best by comparing with them and using their experience<br>Looking for the most effective methods allowing a given business to reach competitive advantage<br>Comparing processes, products, and services with competitors |

Source: A. Bitkowska, G. Wójcik, K. Kolterman. 2010. Koncepcje restrukturyzacji przedsiębiorstw. [In:] Bitkowska A. (ed.) *Procesy restrukturyzacji warunkiem poprawy konkurencyjności przedsiębiorstw*. Warszawa: Difin: 103, M. Źródło–Loda. 2014. *Benchmarking – nowoczesna koncepcja zarządzania organizacją. Prace Naukowo-Dydaktyczne PWSZ im. S.* Pigonia w Krośnie V. 67, Krosno: 204, J. J. Dahlagaard, K. Kristesen, G. K. Kanji. 2000. *Podstawy zarządzania jakością*. Warszawa: Wydawnictwo Naukowe PWN: 208.

The main objects of benchmarking include[96]:

- Products,
- Processes,
- Functions,
- Strategies,
- Costs,
- Organizational structures.

The aims of benchmarking can include[97]:

1. Direct objectives
   - Improved process identification,
   - Referring to other companies,
   - Indicating strengths and weaknesses,
   - Learning from others,
   - Improving operations.
2. Indirect objectives
   - Improving leadership and management skills,
   - Changing the attitude to changes in a company,
   - Increasing customers' satisfaction,
   - Gaining competitive advantage.

Depending on the objectives, different types of benchmarking can be distinguished[98]:

1. Internal:
   - Pros:

---

[96] E. Czyż-Gwiazda. 2006. *Benchmarking. Benchmark Index czyli jak porównywać się z najlepszymi*? Katowice: Centrum Benchmarkingu Polska – TÜV NORD Polska Sp. z o.o.: 11.

[97] J. Nazarko, K. Kuźmicz, E. Szubzda, J. Urban. 2008. *Ogólna koncepcja benchmarkingu i jego stosowalność w szkolnictwie wyższym, w: Benchmarking w systemie szkolnictwa wyższego.* [In:] J. Woźnicki (ed.). Fundacja Rektorów Polskich. Warszawa: 17.

[98] M. Źródło–Loda. 2014. *Benchmarking – nowoczesna koncepcja zarządzania organizacją.* Prace Naukowo-Dydaktyczne PWSZ im. S. Pigonia w Krośnie V. 67. Krosno: 211.

   - Little risk of failure,
   - Easy access to information,
   - Actions aiming at comparing coefficients,
   - Satisfying effects in highly diversified companies,
- Cons:
   - Unwillingness to introduce changes,

2. Competitive:
   - Pros
     - Gaining key information about a company,
     - A possibility to compare processes,
     - Company location – finding its market position,
     - Employee acceptance,
   - Cons
     - Worse access to information,
     - Studies apply to a specific industry,
     - A possibility to follow the solutions used in the industry,
     - Low level of solutions innovation – they are easy to imitate,
3. Functional:
   - Pros
     - A possibility to apply innovations from outside one's industry,
     - Spurring employees to take innovative actions,
   - Cons
     - Problems with the implementation of solutions,
     - High costs and significant time needed for analyzes,
     - Difficult adaptation of the best solutions in the industry to a given company situation.

The process of benchmarking can consist of five stages[99]:

[99] B. Karlöf, S. Stblom. 1995. *Benchmarking – równaj do najlepszych.* Warszawa: Biblioteka Menadżera i Bankowca: 100–103.

1. Planning phase – recognizing the elements to be included in benchmarking (products, services, processes, procedures).
2. Phase of recognizing other participants – indicating who is a point of reference in benchmarking – whether it is a different organizational unit of a company, a competitive organization, or the best company in a given area,
3. Phase of collecting information – it is a very important phase of gathering information, which should be organized in accordance with a precise plan and verified in a defined way. Proper data collection and analysis is crucial in order to correctly conduct a benchmarking process, but some information and data can be difficult or even impossible to access.
4. Analysis phase – collected data is analyzed and used as a basis for taking further steps of implementing changes,
5. Execution phase – changes indicated during the analysis are introduced in the company. It is necessary to establish a hierarchy of changes and their priorities, as well as to evaluate the risk of their implementation.

In order to systematize the process of benchmarking, it can be compared with the Deming Circle (Figure 10), which is connected with continuous improvement of companies in accordance with the PDCA[100] cycle: Plan, Do, Check, Adjust[101].

Benchmarking has numerous advantages, but it also involves certain threats:

- A possibility of copying solutions,
- One cannot cut down their actions in spite of having succeeded,
- There is a slight difference between comparing oneself to other companies and gaining secret and confidential information.

[100] Alternative: Plan, Do, Check, Act.

[101] M. Źródło–Loda. 2014. *Benchmarking – nowoczesna koncepcja zarządzania organizacją*. Prace Naukowo-Dydaktyczne PWSZ im. S. Pigonia w Krośnie V. 67. Krosno: 217.

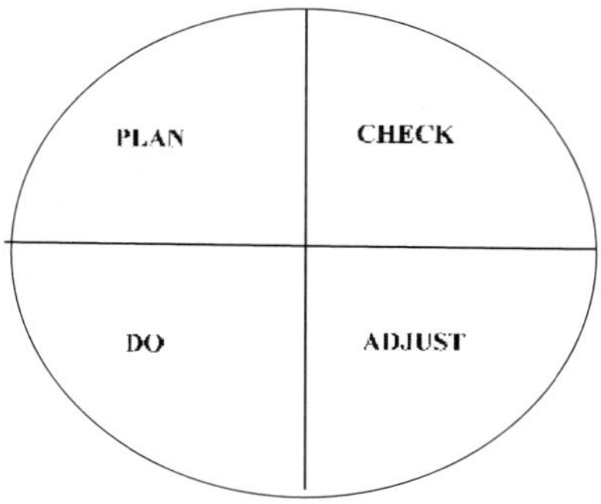


Source: Author's own analysis based on M. Źródło–Loda. 2014. *Benchmarking – nowoczesna koncepcja zarządzania organizacją*. Prace Naukowo-Dydaktyczne PWSZ im. S. Pigonia w Krośnie V. 67. Krosno: 217.

Figure 10. Deming Cycle.

### 2.3.2. Total Quality Management (TQM)

The concept of TQM is based on quality management – a continuous process of striving for perfection of both processes and the way the managers manage the company to maximize customers' satisfaction (Table 10). It is a continuous improvement of one's organization, aiming at satisfying client's needs, which change over time due to the influence of environment, competitors, consumers' behavior.

In the benchmarking process, it is important to know W. E. Deming's studies (Deming Circle), whereas in the quality management process (TQM), we should emphasize the importance of J. M. Juran's approach to improvement and quality increase. Juran created the concept called *Juran's trilogy* based on three elements:

- Quality planning,
- Quality control,
- Quality improvement.

J. M. Juran stresses that 80% of problems with quality in companies are caused by the management, whereas regular employees are responsible for 20% of problems (a so-called *Juran's spiral,* Figure. 11).

**Table 10. Definitions of TQM in Polish and foreign literature**

| Author | Definition |
|---|---|
| A. Hamrol, W. Mantura | TQM is the best possible model of a quality management system, which is created based on complex management through quality and management theories. In fact, instead of implementing TQM, we should always work towards reaching it. |
| M. Sashkin, K. Kiser | Striving for continuous improvement by implementing total quality management in company organizational culture. With the use of applied methods and their standardization, a company aims at reaching customers' satisfaction with their operations with the company. |
| J. J. Bonstingl | TQM is not a concept or a model; it is a lifestyle or a way of thinking. In a company, TQM becomes the aim of company functioning. |
| T. Szucki | TQM is understood as:<br>An integrated process in the whole company. Total Quality Management is executed by all divisions.<br>What is important are customer needs, and not potential and capacities of the company.<br>The aim of company operations directed at the quality management should be known to all employees and organizational units. |

Source: A. Hamrol, W. Mantura. 1998. *Zarządzanie jakością. Teoria i praktyka.* Warszawa, Poznań: Wydawnictwo Naukowe PWN: 354, M. Sashkin, K. J.Kiser. 1993. *Putting Total Quality Management to Work.* San Francisco: Berret-Koehler Publisher: 39, J. J. Bonstingl. 1995. *Szkoły jakości, Wprowadzenie do Total Quality Management w edukacji.* Warszawa: CODN: 16, T. Szucki. 1998. Encyklopedia marketing. Warszawa: Placet.

Quality management in a company was also important for A. V. Feigenbaum, who is a creator of the concept of complex quality control (TQC[102]). Pursuant to this theory, the responsibility for the quality in a company lies with each organizational unit. Proper guidance and control should start with the creation of a company strategy, while focusing on distributing responsibility for the quality of services or products in a company, and aiming at supporting and motivating employees in order to achieve planned and improved quality results in a company.[103]

[102] Total Quality Control.
[103] *A. V. Feigenbaum. 1961. Total Quality Control. New York: McGraw-Hill.*

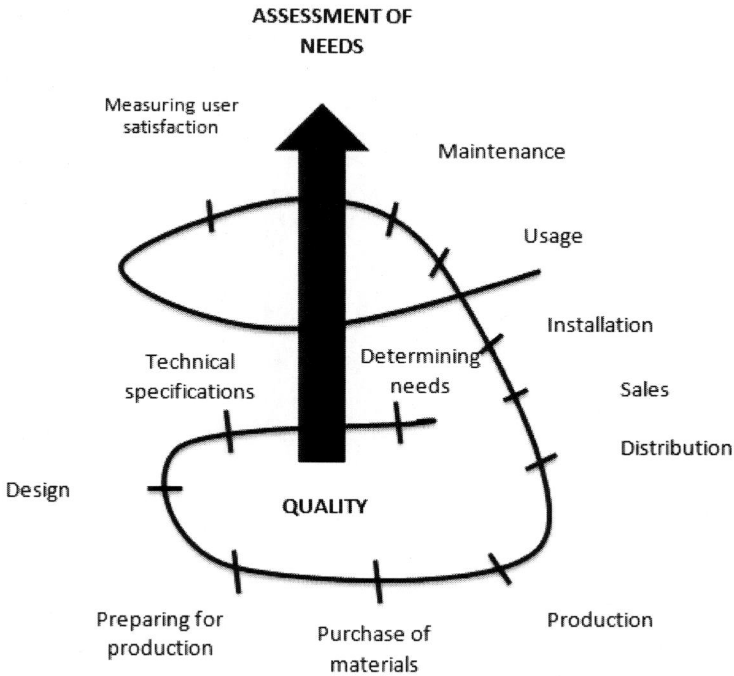


Source: J. Chabiera, S. Doroszewicz, A. Zbierzchowska. 2000. *Zarządzanie jakością. Poradnik menedżera*. Warszawa: Centrum Informacji Menedżera: 11.

Figure 11. J. M. Juran's spiral.

Focus on quality management was also preferred by P. B. Crosby, the creator of a concept of *Quality First.* Crosby stressed that purchasing the highest quality materials and subassemblies, as well as concentrating on the quality of products is always beneficial for the company, because doing something right the first time is cheaper and more effective when it comes to winning customers or new sales markets. There is no need to perform certain actions many times in order to improve offered services, which saves time and reduces costs, as there is no need to pay several times for certain operations, even though their unit prices are lower. What is more, the loss of customers and unused business opportunities are limited; there is also a greater control over possible loss of potential profit. P. B. Crosby created four principles for managers and called them guidelines for managers:

- Quality must be required in execution,
- Prevention is more important than late control,
- Zero errors principle should be a standard rule,
- Evaluation should be performed based on costs of requirements which have not been met, and not on ratios.[104]

The presented concepts represent the main, buy not the only prominent experts in managing companies through quality in the first place. Other contributors include: K. Ishikawa, W. E. Conway, J. S. Oakland.

The concept of TQM is complex and multidimensional, which is a source of many problems when trying to present TQM in a synthetic and comprehensive way. There are many positive characteristics of TQM, but there are also threats related to this concept; which are:

- Time-consuming – the concept of TQM requires time, engagement, and coherence of functioning of company organizational units,
- Labor-intensive – the introduction of TQM requires employees' effort and management's full support. Without managers' support or understanding, TQM can bring more harm than benefits in a business unit,
- Multi-dimensional – managers' and employees' actions should be compliant with the company's strategy and quality policy. Only with such an approach is it possible to achieve positive effects of introduced changes.

### 2.3.3. Lean Management

The main idea is company restructuring resulting from the excessive number of employees versus the executed production, or from company misadjustment to its market situation, as a result of which the organization

---

[104] P. Crosby. 1979. *Quality is Free: The Art. Of Making Quality Certain*. McGraw-Hill.

loses its competitive advantage. What is more, lean management is used in the context of fossilized structures, in a situation when production force is not adapted to the company staff and current trends in the company environment. Such a situation results in wastage and offer misadjustment to the market situation; thus, restructuring is required. It involves simplification of company functioning by changing its activity, eliminating unnecessary costs, eliminating wastage in the form of excessive supplies, or managing the structure of assets by selling those which are unnecessary for the organization core operations[105]. The objectives of lean management mostly include[106]:

- A short production cycle,
- Maximum usage of production force,
- Schedule-compliant cooperation with suppliers,
- Minimized inventory.

Using the concept of lean management in a company can have the following advantages[107]:

- better competitive advantage with cost reduction and higher quality,
- faster decision-making process by limiting management levels leading to making a final decision,
- improved employee motivation.

Apart from benefits, there can also be certain threats connected to lean management[108]:

---

[105] J. P. Womack, D. T. Jones, D. Ross. 2001. *The Machine that Changed the World: The Story of Lean Production*. Harper Collins: 10.

[106] W. M. Grudzewski, I. K. Hejduk. 2004. *Metody projektowania systemów zarządzania*. Warszawa: Difin: 201.

[107] K. Pasternak, B. Grzybowska. 2000. *Metody i techniki zarzadzania w przedsiębiorstwie*. Olsztyn: Wydawnictwo Uniwersytetu Warmińsko – Mazurskiego: 50.

[108] Ibidem: 50.

- possibility of transforming lean management into an ordinary rationalization, which can lead to dismissals and quality deterioration,
- increase of company need for qualified staff and neglecting less-qualified employees.

Lean management uses the process of continuous improvement of products and increased production efficiency (*kaizen*), applying the following tools[109]:

- *SMED*[110], production rationalization – decrease in number of machine changeovers
- *VSM*[111] – controlling the usage of materials in production and providing customers with missing products or product groups,
- simplification of construction, increased standardization,
- *5S* – proper management and effective usage of a workplace,
- *TPM*[112] – ensuring problem-free operation of machines and devices,
- *Six Sigma* – cost reduction and quality improvement by using statistical instruments,
- *Kanban* – production management process,
- *Poka-yoke*[113] – different types of solutions which prevent mistakes and errors,
- Kamishibai[114] – a tool for performing audits,
- A spaghetti diagram – it allows to eliminate improper or unnecessary movement of persons or products,
- *Hoshin kanri* – using a company strategy in all departments,

---

[109] A. Bitkowska, G. Wójcik, K. Kolterman. 2010. *Koncepcje restrukturyzacji przedsiębiorstw*. [In:] Bitkowska A. (ed.). *Procesy restrukturyzacji warunkiem poprawy konkurencyjności przedsiębiorstw*. Warszawa: Difin: 116.

[110] Single Minutes Exchange of Die.

[111] Value stream mapping.

[112] Total Productive Maintenance.

[113] Mistake-Proofing, Error-Proofing.

[114] Kamishibai board.

- *Heijunka*[115] – decreasing inventory without negatively affecting supplies for customers.

In lean management, we use the following concepts:

- Lean thinking – actions aiming at fulfilling customers' needs and ensuring their satisfaction. All actions performed in a company which do not lead to manufacturing products or providing services and which customers want to pay for are perceived as wastefulness[116],
- Just in time – raw and ready materials, as well as other elements necessary for production should be supplied as needed in order to avoid stocking materials and unnecessarily blocking cash flow. Precise synchronization of production and deliveries in order to execute the company strategy and operate more closely with customers,
- MRP – this concept involves a precise process of planning production and minimizing inventory levels. It can be divided into three parts:
  - MRP I – inventory management,
  - MRP II – joined managements of production and inventory levels,
  - MRP III – a detailed schedule of supplies and production materials inventory[117].

## 2.3.4. Outsourcing

It means dividing functions performed by a company and ordering their execution to other business entities. In outsourcing, most functions

---

[115] *Production levelling.*
[116] J. Czerska. 2000. *Lean Production - konieczność, czy możliwość*. Manager 2000, no. 2.
[117] W. M. Grudzewski, I. K. Hejduk. 2004. *Metody projektowania systemów zarządzania*. Warszawa: Difin: 286.

are performed by expert companies and there is no need to employ experts and extend the departments necessary to proper functioning. In such a model, functions are performed better and cheaper[118].

Outsourcing can have the following benefits[119]:

- Reduction of operation costs,
- Focusing on the main business activity, reduced or eliminated dispersion of operations into secondary activities,
- Better performance and higher quality of offered products or services,
- Availability of advanced technologies and innovation.

The objectives of outsourcing can be ordered in the following way[120]:

1. Organizational objectives
    - Better performance,
    - Increased flexibility,
    - Continuous development of the main operations,
    - Increased company value.
2. Development-related objectives
    - Expansion of company operations,
    - Actions aiming at finding new tools and experts to execute company objectives more efficiently,
    - Strengthened competitive advantage of the company,
    - Investment in innovation.
3. Financial objectives
    - Investment reduction,
    - Transferring greater capital to invest in the developments of the main operations.

[118] K. Kolterman. 2008. *Lean production*. Ekonomika i organizacja przedsiębiorstwa, no. 4.

[119] A. Bitkowska, G. Wójcik, K. Kolterman. 2010. *Koncepcje restrukturyzacji przedsiębiorstw* [In:] Bitkowska A. (ed.). *Procesy restrukturyzacji warunkiem poprawy konkurencyjności przedsiębiorstw*. Warszawa: Difin: 118.

[120] M. F. Greaver. 1999. *Strategic Outsourcing. A Structural Approach to Outsourcing Decisions and Initiatives* New York: Amacom: 4-5.

4. Income-related objectives
    - Winning new sales markets,
    - Focus on developing faster than before,
    - Increased achieved margin and sources of income.
5. Cost-related objectives
    - Reduction of the costs of operations other than main operations,
    - Focus on improving financial ratios,
6. Employee-related objectives
    - Increased employee engagement,
    - More accessible career path for the employees.

**Table 11. Types of outsourcing**

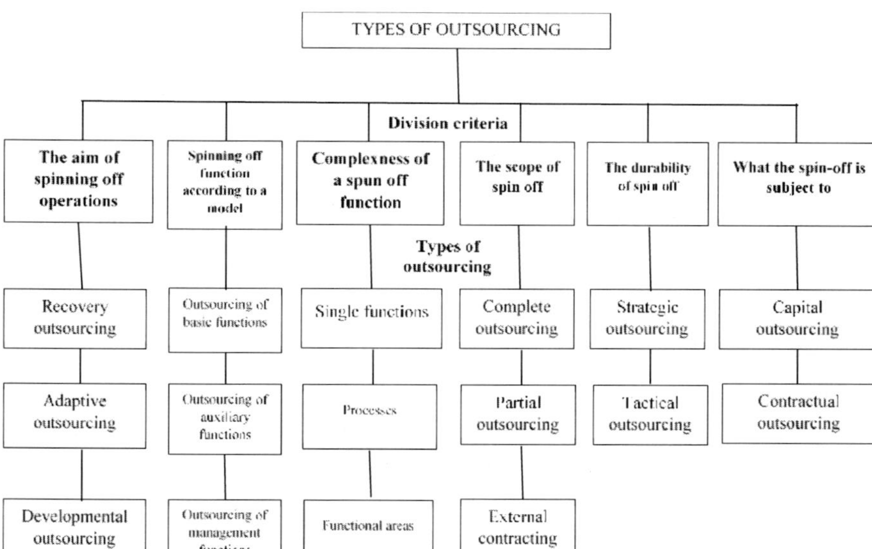


Source: M. Trocki. 2001. Outsourcing. Metoda restrukturyzacji działalności gospodarczej. Warszawa: PWE: 14.

Having listed the objectives, it is important to focus on the types of outsourcing and the criteria of its classification[121]:

[121] M. Trocki. 2001. *Outsourcing. Metoda restrukturyzacji przedsiębiorstw*. Warszawa: PWE: 60.

1. The aim of spinning off operations:
   - Recovery outsourcing,
   - Adaptive outsourcing,
   - Developmental outsourcing.
2. Types of functions:
   - Outsourcing of basic functions,
   - Outsourcing of auxiliary functions,
   - Outsourcing of management functions,
3. The complexity of functions:
   - Single functions,
   - Processes,
   - Functional areas.
4. The scope of spun off areas:
   - Complete outsourcing,
   - Partial outsourcing,
   - External spin off.
5. The durability of spin off:
   - Strategic outsourcing,
   - Tactical outsourcing.
6. What the spin off is subject to:
   - Capital outsourcing,
   - Contractual outsourcing.

There are numerous criteria of dividing outsourcing, therefore also literature names different types of outsourcing (Table 11).

The analysis of outsourcing should include not only benefits but also different types of risks that accompany it. It is crucial to make a decision regarding the elements in a company which will be subject to outsourcing. These can include elements which are necessary for company functioning, and which will be best executed by external entities in such areas as HR management, public relations, or accounting. However, what also should be considered here is whether strategic elements which are decisive for competitive advantage should be spun off in part of in full, or whether they should be executed in the company. A key aspect of outsourcing is how the contract with external entities is constructed – it should be written in a way that is clear and understandable for both parties, with explanation which specific tasks are spun off. The scope of responsibility is crucial for effective functioning of the contracting company and good cooperation with other organizations.

### 2.3.5. Offshoring

Companies which decided to spin off some of their functions to other companies in their country in order to reduce costs and maximize efficiency, search for business partners abroad. The aim is to further reduce costs, since in other countries with specialized staff it is possible to execute the same tasks, but the remuneration for work is lower. Offshoring can be used in two variants:

- Offshoring of services – foreign entities are selected to provide services for a contracting company,
- Offshoring of company management – an effective implementation of an offshoring strategy, so that a given entity executes its business objectives with due diligence and the utmost care for quality, at least within the same scope as it was before the strategy was implemented[122].

Apart from offshoring, there is also offshoring of business processes, which means that corporations commission the provision of services in countries which have a potential in accessing qualified employees. The aim is to ensure the development of corporations and cost reduction at the same time[123]. Creating service centres positively affects the countries in which

[122] D. Ciesielska. 2009. *Offshoring usług. Wpływ na rozwój przedsiębiorstwa*. Warszawa: Wolters Kluwer Polska: 18.
[123] www.paih.gov.pl.

such centres are established, as they contribute to the economic development of their region, leading to an increased demand for experts. What is more, due to foreign investments, corporations compete with one another in specific cities or regions, which is beneficial for the development of both corporations and employees, and, as a consequence, of the whole region or even country.

### 2.3.6. Reengineering

It requires a change in the way a company functions and is managed. It is characterized by a significant, almost revolutionary change of processes, procedures, methods of operating. The way of functioning is designed anew and implemented for the improvement of company operations[124].

The main changes are related to a change in approaching company management. Instead of focusing on functions, it is crucial to concentrate on processes, especially those related to customers and suppliers. What is more, it is important to determine if all processes in a company need to be continued. Next, it is necessary to observe the processes and modify those which are not optimal. Managers should consider a given situation from the customer's perspective and then they will know if the implemented strategy functions correctly[125].

### 2.3.7. Business Unit Segmentation and Spin-Off

It is used in big companies which want to spin off a part of their operations in order to separate secondary structures of their business activity. What is more, such processes take place as a result of actions

---

[124] M. Bednarczyk. 1994. *Zastosowanie koncepcji spin off w przekształceniach przedsiębiorstw państwowych*. Zeszyty Naukowe AE Kraków, no. 444, 5-13.

[125] M. Garstka. 2012. *Restrukturyzacja przedsiębiorstwa – podział przez wydzielenie*. Warszawa: Cedewu: 44.

aiming at creating a transparent organizational structure or when a given company is so developed that it is difficult to manage it. It often happens that spun off departments or organizational units conduct auxiliary business activity and, as a spun off company, especially at the beginning of their operations, cooperate mainly with their mother organization. At that moment, the main task is to aim at extending one's business activity[126].

Spin-off is executed in three stages[127]:

- Listing functions performed in the company,
- Isolating an auxiliary and secondary part of operations and spinning them off to another company with the use of capital and human resources of the mother organization,
- Conducting business activity more rationally and focusing on these operations by separating and spinning off the auxiliary and secondary part of business activity to another company.

### 2.3.8. Downsizing

It is performed by decreasing the size of the company in order to improve its efficiency and profitability. It involves employment reduction and focusing on the main company objective. It often does not require long-time planning, but means a temporary improvement of business situation by affecting costs and allowing to reduce them. Such actions may be applied in a difficult situation of a company, as a method of saving the company from bankruptcy. When we look at the economic environment, cost reduction takes place with a worse position of the market and when trade agreements that are important for company finances are lost[128].

---

[126] Ibidem: 42.

[127] M. Bednarczyk. 1994. *Zastosowane koncepcji spin off w przekształceniach przedsiębiorstw państwowych*, Zeszyty Naukowe AE Kraków, no. 444: 11.

[128] A. Nalepka. 1999. *Restrukturyzacja przedsiębiorstwa. Zarys problematyki.* Warszawa: PWN: 113-147.

### 2.3.9. Outplacement[129]

It is a controlled dismissal of employees and ensuring support in their further professional career. Employers in Poland should report to certain institutions that they intend to dismiss their employees, if the number of persons to be dismissed within 3 months amounts to at least 50 people. Outplacement can be divided into:

- Individual outplacement, which involves dismissing company management or experts. Such employees can shape their further career path with the help of a person specialized in this area: career advisor, image consultant, or a career trainer.
- Group outplacement applicable mostly to employees on operational positions. As a group of employees (and not individually), they receive help in seeking next employment.

## 2.4. The Process of Company Restructuring

The first stage of the restructuring process involves recognizing the company situation. Such an identification requires an analysis of both the company and its environment. Company analysis can include[130]:

- Analysis of an organization,
- Financial analysis,
- Analysis of human resources,
- Analysis of production.

---

[129] Ibidem: 113–147.

[130] Z. Pierścionek. 1995. *Zarządzanie strategiczne w przedsiębiorstwie*. Warszawa: Oficyna Wydawnicza SGH: 119.

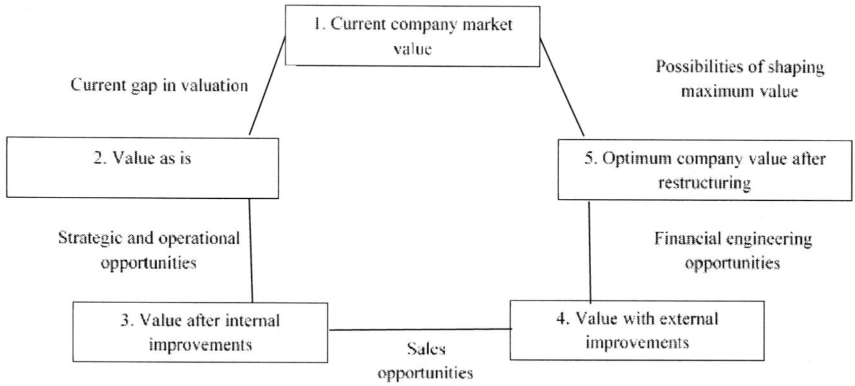


Source: T. Copeland, T. Koller, J. Murrin. *Wycena: mierzenie i kształtowanie wartości firm.* Warszawa 197: WIG-Press: 35.

Figure 12. Restructuring pentagon framework.

When making decisions regarding restructuring, a company can use a suitable plan – a restructuring pentagon framework (Figure 12), taking into consideration the influence of the process on the company value.

A restructuring process should be divided into several stages, which first aim at recognizing the company situation and environment, and then include the preparation of an action plan and the implementation of the company recovery process and improvement of company efficiency (Figure 13).

No every restructuring process is the same. However, it is important to recognize the moment when such a process should start; the way it is conducted depends on the company situation (Figure. 14).

After recognizing that significant changes are needed in a company, it is crucial to perform an economic analysis of operations and the strategy (Figure 15). Based on conclusions drawn from this analysis, a form, scope, and type of restructuring can be chosen.[131]

[131] R. Borowiecki. 1996. *Analiza ekonomiczna jako narzędzie określania obszaru i zakresu działań restrukturyzacyjnych w przedsiębiorstwie.* [In:] R. Borowiecki (ed.). *Restrukturyzacja w procesie przekształceń i rozwoju przedsiębiorstwa.* Kraków: 29-36.

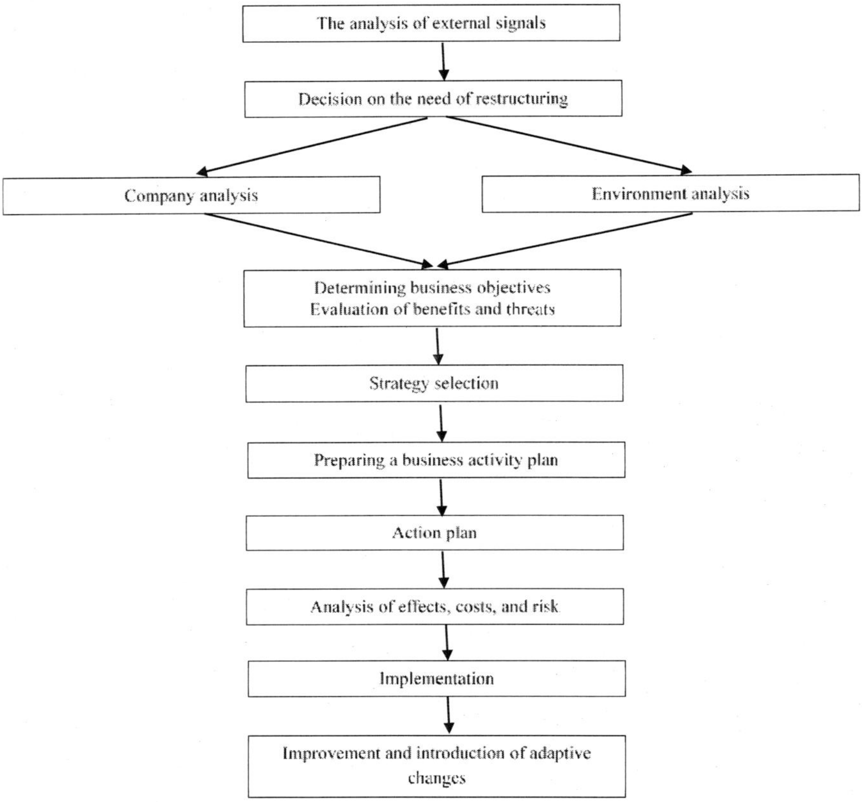


Source: M. Bednarek. 2007. Doskonalenie systemów zarządzania, nowa droga do przedsiębiorstwa lean. Warszawa: Difin: 65.

Figure 13. Diagram of a restructuring process.

After deciding to conduct a restructuring process, a company needs to perform a strategic analysis of resources and potential. The following methods can be used:

- Company strategic balance – there are twelve decisive elements for the management system[132]:
    1. Cooperation with the environment,
    2. Technology and organization of production,

[132] H. Bieniok, J. Marek. 1999. *Kompleksowa metoda diagnozowania systemu zarządzania przedsiębiorstwa*. Katowice: AE.

3. Strategic plan of product development,
4. Product distribution method,
5. Means of communicating with the environment (promotion and marketing),
6. Financial matters – financial result, profitability, margin,
7. Price shaping method,
8. Planning of tasks and processes,
9. Human resources management,
10. Fixed assets management,
11. Materials management,
12. Internal factors characterizing a company,

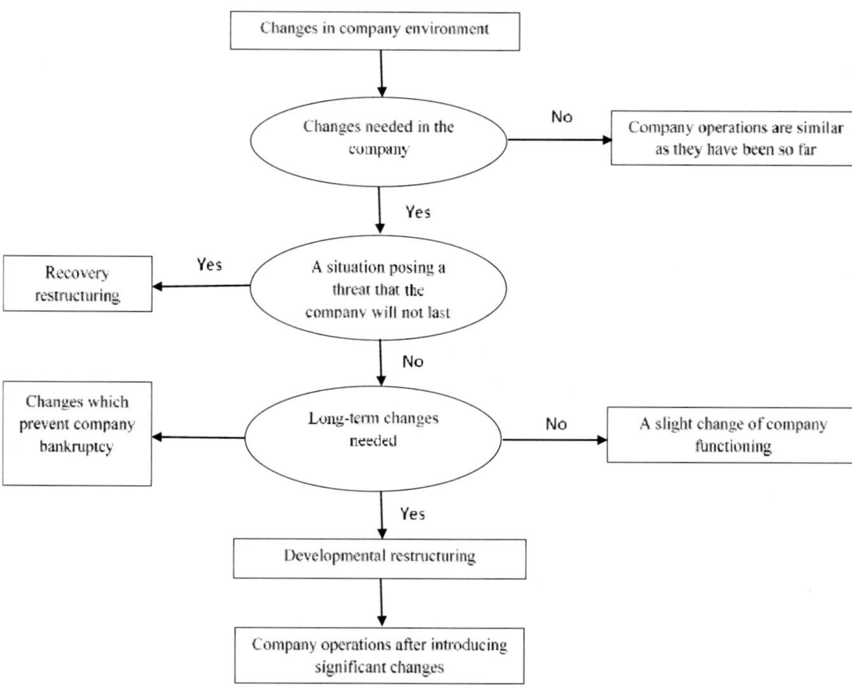


Source: A. Nalepka. 1999. Restrukturyzacja przedsiębiorstwa. Zarys problematyki. Kraków: PWN: 26.

Figure 14. Restructuring in the process of introducing changes in a company.

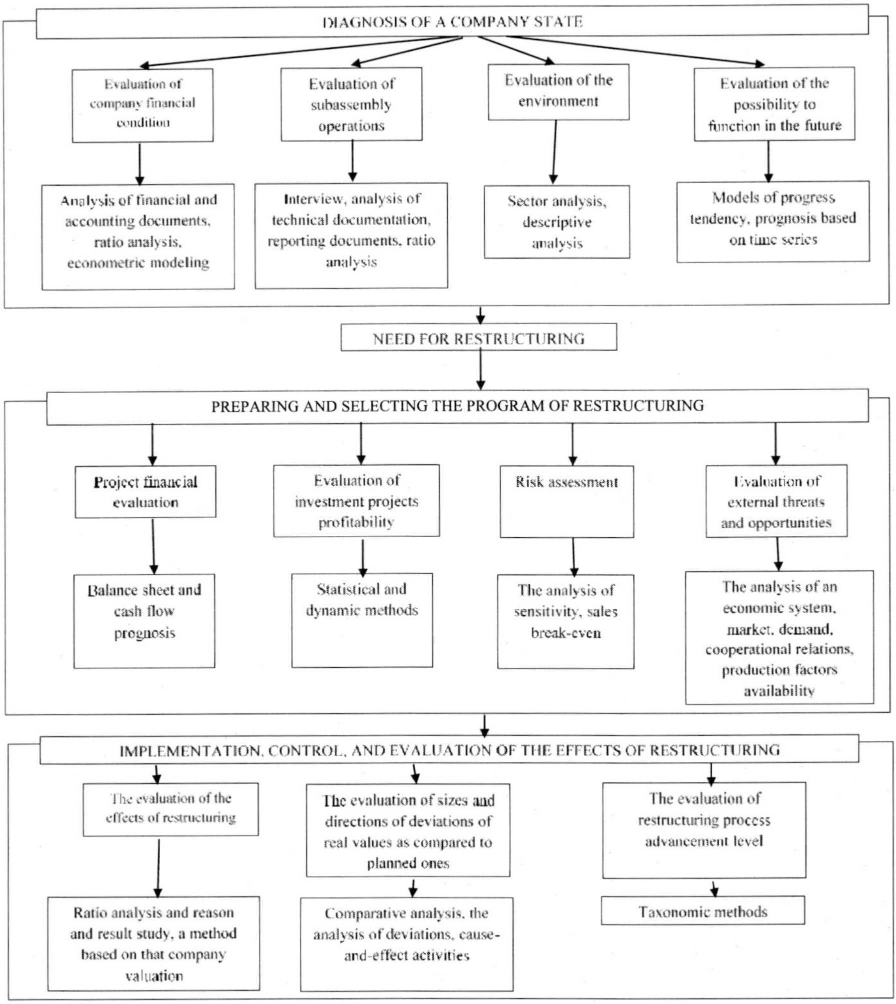


Source: E. Wysłocka. 2004. Zarządzanie restrukturyzacja przedsiębiorstwa, a metody analizy ekonomicznej. [In:] Cz. Glinkowski (ed). Zarządzanie zmianą. Kierunki i efektywność restrukturyzacji sprywatyzowanych przedsiębiorstw w Polsce. Warszawa: 83-99.

Figure 15. Economic analysis in the context of a restructuring process.

- The analysis of key success factors – the evaluation of a company situation focusing on selecting the main factors which are considered the most important. They include[133]:
  - Factors influencing product and technology development
    - Opportunities and success related to one's activity in research and development (R&D),
    - The ability to create new products, especially innovative ones,
    - The ability to implement and properly use new technologies,
    - Proper cooperation with suppliers and recipients, leading to effective functioning and possibly faster company development,
  - Production-related factors
    - Quality control of manufactured products,
    - Actions aiming at maximum usage of production force, which will contribute to beneficial distribution of fixed costs per a production unit,
    - A possibility to make quick changes in the production structure in order to adapt to market requirements,
    - Company position guaranteeing relatively easy access to production factors,
  - Sales-related factors
    - Ability of company to manufacture products in accordance with customer preferences,
    - Proper creation of a product selection,
    - Possible diverse payment options,
    - Access to distribution channels,
    - The way product price policy is shaped,
    - *Public relations* operations including product promotion methods, selection of channels for communicating with customers,

---

[133] T. Gołębiowski. 2001. *Zarządzanie strategiczne, planowanie i kontrola*. Warszawa: Difin: 152-153.

    - The ability to win customers' loyalty,
  - Other factors
    - A selected method of negotiating with suppliers,
    - An ability to find financing sources on standard or non-standard background:
      - Bank loans or alternative financing like: mezzanine capital[134] or crowdfunding[135]
    - An ability to attract and employ highly qualified employees,
    - A well-functioning system of motivating employees.
- Value chain analysis – a strategic model of company diagnosis proposed by M. E. Porter. Value chain analysis means recognizing and ensuring better functioning of operations aiming at convincing customers to see a specific product as valuable[136]. The main tasks include[137]:
  - The analysis of previous cooperation with customers – identification of the course of previous cooperation, emphasizing advantages and isolating elements which can be improved,
  - The analysis of executed company functions – recognition of the executed functions and their execution methods divided into processes and patterns. It is crucial to prioritize functions in order to select those which are the most important,
  - The analysis of costs and losses – recognizing which factors lead to worse efficiency or excessive costs,
  - Recovery actions – showing the areas in which the company and its processes should be streamlined. It is important to

---

[134] Kuryłek Z. 2015. *Mezzanine Capital. Nowoczesne finansowanie przedsiębiorstw,* CeDeWu, Warszawa.

[135] Motylska – Kuźma, A. 2018. *Alternative finance and sustainable development.* The Central European Review of Economics and Management, 2(1): 175-187.

[136] G. Gierszewska, M. Romanowska. 2003. *Analiza strategiczna przedsiębiorstwa.* Warszawa: PWN: 173.

[137] J. Filipczuk. 2004. *Analiza strategiczna przedsiębiorstwa, Teoria i praktyka.* Sochaczew: WSZiM: 107–110.

determine the strategy of executing recovery actions, and then of controlling their execution.

**Table 12. Stages of restructuring and its effects**

| Stages of restructuring | Restructuring methods and instruments | Effects of restructuring |
|---|---|---|
| Stage I | • Improvement of communication between the market and a company<br>• Own share redemption by a company | • Elimination of information gap<br>• Improvement in the perceptions of the company as an innovative object |
| Stage II | • Reengineering<br>• TQM<br>• Lean Management<br>• Benchmarking<br>• Just In Time<br>• Kaizen<br>• Downsizing<br>• Change of the structure of organization<br>• Change in the remuneration system<br>• Strategic alliances | • Improved company asset management<br>• Quality improvement<br>• Work performance improvement<br>• Sales dynamics increase<br>• Increase of achieved margin |
| Stage III | • Mergers and acquisitions (M&A)<br>• Outsourcing<br>• Outplacement<br>• Insourcing<br>• Spin-off<br>• Investments<br>• Divestments | • Change in company asset structure<br>• Company operations diversification<br>• Company operations specialization<br>• Usage of synergy effects |
| Stage IV | • Leveraged buyout (LBO)<br>• Management buyout (MBO)<br>• Privatization<br>• Redemption of own shares | • Capital structure optimization<br>• Using the financial leverage effect<br>• Using a tax shield<br>• Changes in the ownership structure |

Source: R. Borowiecki, E. Wysłocka. 2012. *Analiza Ekonomiczna i ocena ekspercka w procesie restrukturyzacji przedsiębiorstw*. Warszawa: Difin: 67.

**Table 13. The effects of restructuring**

| Effects | Recovery restructuring | Adaptive restructuring | Developmental restructuring |
|---|---|---|---|
| Financial | • Increase of revenues and cost reduction<br>• Debt removal<br>• Liquidity improvement | • Financial results improvement<br>• Maintaining good financial condition | • Financial condition improvement<br>• Mergers and acquisitions |
| Technological | • Better usage of production factors | • Product quality improvement<br>• Technology improvement<br>• Introduction of new products | • Investment in new products<br>• Better production organization |
| Marketing | • New forms and channels of sale<br>• Extended sales network | • Market development<br>• Product development | • Introduction of new products<br>• Better sales management |

Source: W. Gabrusewicz. 1999. Restrukturyzacja przedsiębiorstw i metody oceny jej efektów. *Przegląd Organizacji* 3/1999: 26-29.

The next stage is the evaluation of the company strategic position, conducted as a combination of environment analysis with the examination of company potential[138]. The following methods can be distinguished:

1. Portfolio methods – the analysis of the company market situation in the form of a matrix of factors divided into those controlled by the company and those not:
   - BCG-matrix,
   - Technological portfolio,
   - McKinsey-portfolio,
   - ADL matrix,
   - Hofer matrix,

[138] J. Filipczuk. 2004. *Analiza strategiczna przedsiębiorstwa, Teoria i praktyka*. Sochaczew: WSZiM: 145.

2. SWOT analysis – recognizing four groups of factors, divided into the following: strengths, weaknesses, opportunities, and threats.

Different restructuring instruments and methods can be used at different stages and lead to positive effects of this process (Table 12).

The effects of restructuring can be analyzed in three dimensions: as financial, technological, and marketing effects (Table 13).

A taxonomic restructuring coefficient[139] based on D. Strahl's[140] taxonomic method allows to evaluate how advanced the restructuring process is. The evaluation was performed with the use of eight coefficients categorized into four groups[141]:

1. Property-related restructuring:
   - $X_1^M$ – a ratio of share of investment expenditures in the value of sold products (a stimulant[142]),
   - $X_2^M$ – assets turnover ratio = sold products value/value of fixed and current assets (a stimulant),
2. Product-related restructuring:
   - $X_1^P$ – sales profitability ratio = profit/loss on sales/revenue value (a stimulant),
   - $X_2^P$ – share of export in sold products = value of products for export/value of sold products (a stimulant),
3. Organizational restructuring:
   - $X_1^Z$ – inventory rotation ratio in days (an inhibitor[143]),
   - $X_2^Z$ – debt collection ratio in days (an inhibitor),

---

139 Elaborated in the Institute of Economic Sciences of the Polish Academy of Sciences (INE PAN).

140 D. Strahl. 1990. *Metody programowania rozwoju społeczno-gospodarczego.* Warszawa: PWE: 1990.

141 S. Krajewski, P. Kaczorowski. 1999. *Taksonomiczny wskaźnik restrukturyzacji*, *Working Papers,* no. 27. Warszawa: INE PAN. P. Kaczorowski, A. Stępniak-Kucharska. *Próba oszacowania taksonomicznego wskaźnika restrukturyzacji, Working Papers* no. 16. Warszawa: INE PAN.

142 The increase of this value informs about positive changes.

143 The decrease in value informs about positive changes.

4. Financial restructuring:
   - $X_1^F$ – current liquidity ratio = current assets/current liabilities (a nominant[144]),
   - $X_2^F$ – a ratio of relations between liabilities and sales own cost (an inhibitor).

The elements of diagnostic characteristics matrices were normalized, with the direction of relations between a restructuring level to the measure value taken into consideration. The values of ratios were reduced to the value of <0;1> which allowed for their comparison. The matrices of characteristics allowed to calculate component taxonomic coefficients in four groups of restructuring. They were calculated as an arithmetic average of normalized component coefficients assigned to four groups of restructuring. The following component synthetic coefficients were created:

- Property-related restructuring ($W^M$),
- Product-related restructuring ($W^P$),
- Operational restructuring ($W^Z$),
- Financial restructuring ($W^F$)[145].

A taxonomic restructuring coefficient (*taksonomiczny wskaźnik restrukturyzacji*, TWR) is a geometric average of four component coefficients[146]:

$$TWR^t_k = \sqrt[4]{WM * WP * WZ * WF}$$

- TWR close to 1 – proper adaptation to changeable external conditions, effective management of company resources.
- TWR close to 0 – no adaptation to market requirements.

---

[144] There is a reference value which is optimal.

[145] R. Borowiecki, E. Wysłocka. 2012. *Analiza ekonomiczna i ocena ekspercka w procesie restrukturyzacji przedsiębiorstw*. Warszawa: Difin: 152.

[146] Ibidem: 151.

The effects of restructuring can be diverse, but they should result in the improvement of company functioning efficiency understood as the improvement of the quality of offered products, work conditions, and staff motivation, as greater diversification and importance of products for customers, and as numerous channels of customers communicating with a company[147]. All these elements should lead to the improvement of net revenues from sales, achieved gross margin from sales, achieved operating profit, to the optimization of owned capital structure, and to the improvement of achieved net financial result. Before making a decision about starting restructuring, it is important to analyze this process based on the examples of other companies in which restructuring was successful.

## 2.5. Restructuring in Business Practice

The restructuring process was conducted in numerous companies in Poland, with many successful cases of execution.

### 2.5.1. Restructuring in PHPU Arkol sp. z o. o.[148]

#### *2.5.1.1. Company Operations*

The basic operations of the company include production, trade, and services related to furniture manufacturing for big chain customers and small recipients. Throughout the years, the company has expanded its operations, offering furniture for offices, hotels, and stores, but also custom-made pieces and furniture for retail customers. The company has strategic customers known on the Polish and global markets, including:

---

[147] More about decision making in company can be found in: A. Motylska – Kuźma, J. Wieprow. 2017. *Psychologiczne aspekty podejmowania decyzji finansowych w przedsiębiorstwie*, Szczecin, Zeszyty Naukowe Uniwersytetu Szczecińskiego, Finanse, Rynki Finansowe, Ubezpieczenia nr 1/2017 (85): 129-139.

[148] K. Kolterman. 2010. *Restrukturyzacja poprzez transfer technologii na przykładzie PHPU Arkol sp. z o.o.* [In:] Bitkowska A. (ed.). *Procesy restrukturyzacji warunkiem poprawy konkurencyjności przedsiębiorstw*. Warszawa: Difin: 209.

- Banks,
- Shopping centres,
- Offices.

Initially, in the mid-1990s, the company developed successfully due to the lack of market saturation. After a number of years, the situation changed due to the significant increase of prices of real property to buy or rent in Warsaw. Companies used space necessary to conduct their main operations. Thus, the demand for furniture was limited, and the furniture in private houses of retail customers changed once every several years. What is more, many products were imported, and their quality was better than the quality of Polish products, which resulted from the lack of proper manufacturing technology.

### *2.5.1.2. Restructuring – Technology Transfer*

The company management board made a decision to implement changes in order to achieve and maintain better competitive advantage as well as increase the earning capacity of their business activity via investments in new production technologies. The whole process was redesigned and included:

- Technology transfer:
  - An advanced machine park,
  - New materials for production,
  - A change of the production process,
- Change in company management:
  - Performance increase and less work needed,
  - Management structure simplification,
  - Quality increase,
  - Using *marketing – mix*.

Furthermore, the following management methods were chosen: *lean management*, *lean production, just in time, customer relationship management* (CRM), and *outsourcing* of selected services, including: legal services, cleaning services, repairs, catering, market monitoring and research.

A key element in the restructuring process was the usage of a new production line, which led to the following changes in the company:

- Product selection diversification,
- Using advanced production materials,
- Increased diversity in the manufactured product offer,
- Decreased employment,
- Increased performance calculated per one employee,
- Product price reduction with the increase of return/profitability,
- Ordering and controlling processes in a company,
- Cost reduction of company operations,
- Higher quality and flow of documents.

## 2.5.2. Restructuring in *Centrum Edukacji* EDUS[149]

### *2.5.2.1. Company Operations*

The activity of educational institutions depends on the number of their students. The current demographic situation in Poland is rather unfavorable. Fewer students means lower subsidies and the need to take restructuring actions.

Centrum Edukacji EDUS (EDUC Education Center) is a private educational institution with the status of a public school specializing in general and vocational education. The company ensures effective and proven teaching methods based on many years of experience as well as qualified staff. The main operations include organizing trainings for companies and institutions. Monitoring the situation of environment,

[149] G. Wójcik. 2010. *Restrukturyzacja firmy szkoleniowej Centrum Edukacji EDUS.* [In:] Bitkowska A. (ed.). *Procesy restrukturyzacji warunkiem poprawy konkurencyjności przedsiębiorstw*. Warszaw: Difin: 217.

working towards the continuous development and reinforcing business strengths, as well as eliminating weaknesses allowed to create a corporate strategy and make a decision to perform company restructuring.

### *2.5.2.2. Restructuring – Recovery and Developmental Character*

The process of restructuring included the analysis of environment and the internal situation of the company. The following factors were taken into consideration:

- The growth dynamics of gross national product,
- Inflation level,
- Low level of debt,
- Advantageous financial conditions in banks.

Apart from these factors, a SWOT analysis was performed.

The criterion of recovery and developmental restructuring was its added value. In general, its aim was to increase the market value by improving the efficiency of operations.

The restructuring process led to the change of the organizational structure, directed on increasing the level of satisfying the market and customers' needs.

The recovery restructuring involved increasing the quality of services, development of employees, and introduction of a motivational system.

The developmental restructuring was based on extending the company business activity by using new teaching methods and techniques, obtaining new certificates, starting a cooperation with university teachers. In general, the building was refurbished, adding new lecture rooms and labs. The company used outsourcing in the area of accounting and cleaning services.

The recovery and developmental restructuring resulted in the improvement of functioning, increase of flexibility, and motivation to be innovative.

## 2.5.3. Restructuring in *Biuro Projektów Telekomunikacyjnych*[150]

### *2.5.3.1. Company Operations*

Within its activity, the company prepares documentation for the construction or modernization of technical infrastructure for telecommunication. The company operations are based on internal procedures guaranteeing the quality of provided services. The company does not have an ISO certificate, and its industry experienced an increase of competition, especially of global entities which buy out existing national-level companies, capitalize them, and introduce advanced technologies. Thus, smaller organization have to agree on cooperating with bigger partners or find their niche where they can be competitive through their flexibility in operations.

Biuro Projektów Telekomunikacyjnych provided services for telecommunication, and then, as a result of a changing situation in its environment, it focused on services for road construction companies. It required that the company changed its approach to the design process and introduced new procedures for advanced business solutions that streamline functioning and work.

### *2.5.3.2. Process Restructuring*

The process mostly included restructuring of processes in the company, with a focus on the Deming diagram and ARIS concept. The main idea was to create an organization which is able to adapt to the customer's needs – a "learning" company. What is more, the processes were simplified and decreased in number. The company structure did not change as it is very limited, and the changes were introduced mostly in the area of processes. Process orientation includes:

---

150 S. Olszewski. 2010. *Restrukturyzacja procesów na przykładzie Biura Projektów Telekomunikacyjnych.* [In:] Bitkowska A. (ed.) *Procesy restrukturyzacji warunkiem poprawy konkurencyjności przedsiębiorstw.* Warszawa: Difin: 223.

- Focusing on the quality of executed projects,
- Mutual cooperation between groups,
- Focusing on system-oriented perspective,
- Focusing on customer satisfaction.

The effect was the increase of quality of provided services, reduction of time needed to execute tasks and, as a result, the whole project, due to advanced technologies and focus on innovation. Such actions allowed the company to develop and cooperate with big companies. The restructuring process led to the stabilization of the company situation over the years and allowed it to continue developing.

## 2.5.4. Restructuring in *PKO Bank Polski SA*[151]

### *2.5.4.1. Company Operations*

The world financial crisis and the slowdown in the Polish economy affected bank operation, especially their financial results. Financial institutions, including banks, significantly affect the economy, providing sources of financing, and gather the society's savings. Banks are a foundation supporting the economy which could not function without them.

The main competitors of the bank are all financial institutions in Poland and in the region of Central and Eastern Europe.

### *2.5.4.2. Technological and Process Restructuring*

The main task of the bank was to create a new strategy aiming at changing and modernizing processes, methods related to the section of retail banking. The task was to transform the bank into a flourishing institution using technological novelties in its operation.

The aim of restructuring was to:

---

[151] P. Kawiński. 2010. *Restrukturyzacja pionu bankowości detalicznej PKO Banku Polskiego SA*. [In:] Bitkowska A. (ed.). *Procesy restrukturyzacji warunkiem poprawy konkurencyjności przedsiębiorstw*. Warszawa: Difin: 233.

- Allow the bank to regain its market leader position,
- Change and improve the image of the bank,
- Increase the attractiveness of the product offer,
- Allow for a dynamic development of electronic banking,
- Increase efficiency,
- Lead to innovative operations.

A new strategy included a strong customer-orientation approach, dividing customers into different distribution channels according to a criterion of cash flow to their accounts. The bank offer for regular customers was improved by using loyalty programs. The product diversification was increased by extending the selection of previously available products and services by new ones, such as different types of insurance: property-related ones, third-party liability insurance, and life insurance options. Apart from that, the employee motivation system was changed with material and non-material motivation elements. What is more, a new system of employee annual evaluation was introduced. There was also an idea for a possible cost reduction by using outsourcing services in certain non-strategic areas of bank operations and for intensive product promotion in the form of marketing. The implementation process took 1.5 year. The effect of restructuring was mostly the increase of customer satisfaction, better contact, and elimination of the need to visit the bank offices due to the electronic access to the bank channels. The effects were measured with the use of a market study of customers' satisfaction.

## 2.5.5. Restructuring in *Volkswagen*[152]

### *2.5.5.1. Company Operations*

Volkswagen is an international concern manufacturing cars. Car production in the European constitutes 27% of the world production. Due

---

[152] K. A. Wójcik. 2010. *Restrukturyzacja na przykładzie koncernu Volkswagen.* [In:] Bitkowska A. (ed.). *Procesy restrukturyzacji warunkiem poprawy konkurencyjności przedsiębiorstw.* Warszawa: Difin: 223.

to the developing globalization and the need to maintain or even improve the company competitive advantage, Volkswagen decided to execute a restructuring process called *ForMotion,* which took two years. Its effects did not satisfy the management board, so the next restructuring program – *ForMotion plus* – started.

### *2.5.5.2. Multidimensional (Recovery, Developmental, and Process) Restructuring*

The aim of restructuring was to improve processes related to managing a huge concern, to reduce production costs, and maximize profits. The task was to reduce long-term costs and increase employee awareness about the company situation and how they can affect the future of the company. Thus, non-material values affected real material valuables. What is more, company processes were isolated and streamlined or eliminated, if they unnecessarily prolonged the production process. Restructuring involved listing many stages for which specific managers were responsible. The sole decision to perform restructuring was very important, but the effects of changes and their measurement method were also crucial. Streamlining processes resulted in the improvement of functioning efficiency and the increase of work performance. The effects were visible after a short time, and generated net loss changed into net profit in the year that followed the restructuring process. Furthermore, the production lines were changed and used in the production of different brands offered by Volkswagen in its portfolio. Also, informing employees about the results of restructuring and next challenges streamlined the process of introducing change, which were easily implemented, and the awareness of the objective motivated employees.

The executed restructuring in a big concern was a complicated and multidimensional process, due to the company business engagement in many parts of the world. The division into stages and careful change tracking led to success in many aspects of operations and truly improved the sales and achieved net profit.

*Chapter 3*

# Restructuring Process in Wratislavia Bio Sp. z o.o. – A Case Study

## 3.1. Characteristics of Wratislavia Bio Sp. z o.o. and the Industry in Which It Operates

Wratislavia Bio Sp. z o.o. is one of the biggest companies producing methyl esters of higher fatty acids and pharmaceutical glycerine in Poland. The strategy of the management board was to build a company operating at least on the European level, or even globally, within the area of renewable sources of energy, which would continue to develop and manufacture products needed on the Polish and global markets. These actions aimed at achieving the best competitive advantage, a significant share in the market, and the improvement of sales profit and financial result.

### 3.1.1. Vision, Mission, and Objectives to Achieve

The basic object of the company operations is biofuel production. The production installations have the performance of 150 thousand tons of methyl esters (biodiesel), 15 thousand tons of glycerine (a side product), and 60 thousand tons of bioethanol per year. This makes the company one of the leaders of biodiesel production in Poland. The production is directed mostly to corporations from the fuel industry, operating on the Polish market – PKN Orlen and Grupa LOTOS. The production plant is located in Wrocław. What is more, the company also uses its warehouses to sell colza oil.

The company aims at developing the industry of biofuels, and especially at taking new roads in their development and implementing solutions which are innovative at both the European and global level, taking into consideration the production and environmental protection.

The company mission is to produce fuel and provide it to the main recipients in Poland, Europe, and in the world, in compliance with the rules of sustainable development.

The main objectives of the company include:

- Providing enough biocomponents for refineries
- Increasing competitive advantage nationally and abroad
- Creating advanced solutions which are models in the industry

### 3.1.2. Basic Products of the Company

Basic products offered by the company include:

#### *3.1.2.1. Methyl Esters of Fatty Acids*

They are formed as a result of the transesterification reaction of vegetable oils or animal fats with methanol. Thanks to its physical and chemical properties, they serve as an alternative for diesel fuel and can be used to power cars with a compression-ignition (diesel) engine as a pure oil or a combustible mixture with diesel fuel (B5, B20, etc.). Wratislavia-Bio Sp. z o.o. produces esters purely based on colza oil. In such a case, such esters are called RMEs (Rapeseed Methyl Esters), which are characterized by the highest quality among this type of products and meet the requirements of the EN 14214 standard.

### *3.1.2.2. Raw Glycerine*

Glycerine is the main side product of the transesterification reaction. Thus, the company obtains raw glycerine in the production of biodiesel. It is the simplest propyl trihydride alcohol. Raw glycerine is currently widely used, starting from heating industry (as a fuel used in boilers) to fertilizer and fodder industry. Nowadays, raw glycerin is mostly processed in order to obtain refined glycerine of pharmaceutical quality.

### *3.1.2.3. Pharmaceutical Glycerine*

Refined glycerine is created as a result of refining raw glycerine. In the production of refined glycerine, the company uses only raw glycerine obtained from colza oil which was not genetically modified. Refined glycerine is widely used in the food and pharmaceutical industry.

### *3.1.2.4. Bioethanol*

It is an anhydrous ethyl alcohol (ethanol fuel) obtained from products of plant origin. It is used in the petroleum industry as an ecological biocomponent of engine fuels and a component for the production of ethyl tert-butyl ether (ETBE). Adding bioethanol to engine fuels leads to a significant decrease of the content of greenhouse gases in exhaust fumes. The increasingly wider usage of renewable sources of energy, and bioethanol among them, allows to reduce the usage of fossil fuels, the resources of which are limited. Thanks to its properties, bioethanol can become one of the most important materials serving as the source of energy in the future.

### *3.1.2.5. Colza Oil*

Due to its basic operations of producing methyl esters, Wratislavia Bio Sp. z o.o. has an access to the market of colza oil both in Poland and the rest of Europe. Big volumes of this product allow for successful reduction of purchase costs and obtaining huge volumes. Thanks to that it is also possible to sell colza oil with a proper business margin. What is more, with company production force, it is possible to produce colza oil of higher quality than the oil offered on the market. Such production involves processing products of worse quality (raw oil) with the use of owned installations for refining oil to higher quality products, highly demanded on the market.

### 3.1.3. Industry Characteristics

In order to present the way the industry of the company functions, it is important to explain the key terms characterizing the market of biofuels:

- Liquid biofuels – benzines containing more than 5% biocomponents or more than 15% esters and diesel with more than 7% biocomponents; ester, bioethanol, biomethanol, dimethyl ether, and pure plant oil – pure fuel, biogas obtained from biomass;
- Biocomponents – bioethanol, biomethanol, ester, dimethyl ether, pure plant oil, and synthetic hydrocarbons;
- Bioethanol – ethyl alcohol produced from biomass (added to benzines);
- Biodiesel – methyl ester produced from plant or animal oil (added to diesel fuel);
- B100 – biofuel produced on the basis of plant oils intended for vehicles with a diesel engine (96.5% of methyl esters).

Apart from understanding the terms which are important from the perspective of operating in this industry, for proper functioning it is also necessary to recognize which generation of biofuels is important at a given time and, possibly, which generations will be introduced in the following years (Figure 16). The aim of the company is to maintain competitive advantage and, in the future, to develop by increasing production, deliveries, and, in a long-term perspective, the market share of the company.

Poland is an important market which produces renewable sources of energy in the form of biocomponents (Table 14).

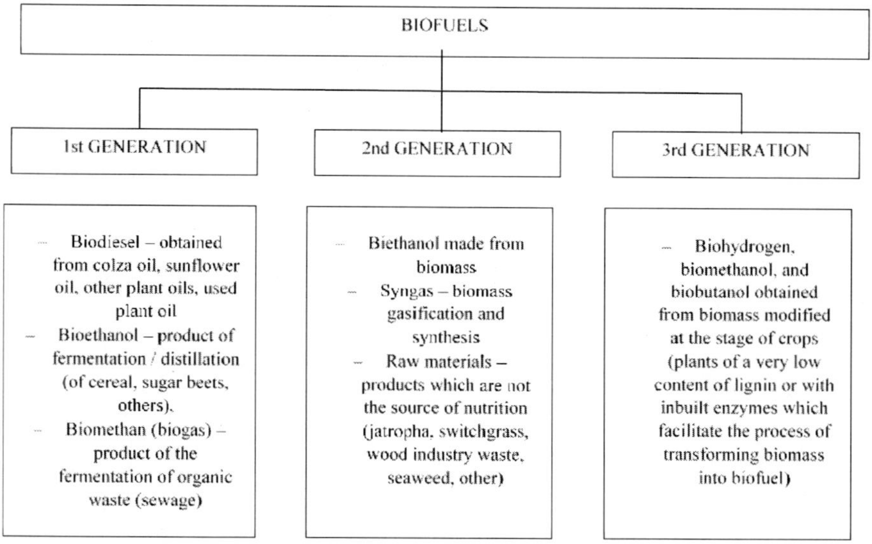


Source: Act on biocomponents and liquid biofuels of 25 August 2006 (Dz. U. [*Journal of Laws*] of 2006 No. 169 item 1199).

Figure 16. Generations of biofuels.

## Table 14. The main producers of biocomponents in Europe

| **Country** | **Bioethanol [mln t]** | **Biodiesel** [mln t] | **Total production [mln t]** | **Total production [ktoe*]** |
|---|---|---|---|---|
| Germany | 0.6 | 2 524 | 2 525 | 2 647 |
| France | 1 | 1 948 | 1 949 | 2 383 |
| Spain | 0.4 | 854 | 854 | 1 003 |
| Poland | 0.1 | 330 | 330 | 381 |
| Total in the world | 58.4 | 15 831 | 15 890 | 51 769 |
| Total in EU | 2.3 | 7 711 | 7 713 | 9 954 |

Source: Biofuels Platform 2010.

**Table 15. Consumption of biofuels in selected countries of EU (ktoe*)**

| Country | Bioethanol | Biodiesel | Other | Total consumption |
|---|---|---|---|---|
| Germany | 751 | 2 235 | 54 | 3 040 |
| France | 254 | 1 788 | 0 | 2 042 |
| Italy | 156 | 1 297 | 0 | 1 453 |
| Spain | 234 | 1 187 | 0 | 1 420 |
| Great Britain | 317 | 827 | 0 | 1 143 |
| Poland | 154 | 790 | 35 | 977 |
| Austria | 69 | 408 | 13 | 490 |
| Sweden | 191 | 175 | 46 | 412 |
| Belgium | 50 | 277 | 0 | 327 |
| Portugal | 0 | 325 | 0 | 325 |
| Total in EU 27 | 2 689 | 10 344 | 150 | 13 179 |

Source: *EurObsev'ER* 2012; * Tonne of oil equivalent (ktoe) – energy equivalent of one metric tonne of petroleum with net caloric value of 10,000 kcal/kg.

Apart from production, it is also important to consider the consumption of biofuels in the selected countries of EU, expressed in ktoe* (Table 15).

### 3.1.4. The Outline of Business Activity in the Biofuel Industry

Legal basis for the regulation of biofuels market in the Community was established mainly with two legal acts: Directive 2003/30/EC of the European Parliament and of the Council of 8 May 2003 on the promotion of the use of biofuels or other renewable fuels for transport and with Directive 2003/96/EC of the Council of the European Union of 27 October 2003 restructuring the Community framework for the taxation of energy products and electricity. Directive of 2009 on the energy from renewable sources requires that the sector of transport reaches a 10-percent share of energy coming from renewable sources to 2020; the directive on the quality of fuels determined the aim of limiting greenhouse gases emission caused by fuels used in the sector of transport by 6 percent by 2020. It is foreseen that biofuels will significantly contribute to the achievement of these aims. The policy of the European Union countries aims at limiting the emission of greenhouse gases to the atmosphere and decreasing the share of fossil fuels used in the production of electricity and in the means of transport. Responding to the European Union regulations, based on the Act of 25 August 2006 on biocomponents and liquid biofuels (Journal of Laws No. 169, item 1199, as amended), Polish law provides for that, starting from 2008, the producers and intermediaries in the sale of liquid biofuels are obliged to ensure a minimum share of biocomponents and other renewable fuels in a total amount of sold fuels in a given year (this ratio is called *Narodowy Cel Wskaźnikowy* – NCW, National Index Target). A minimum share of biocomponents is counted as per its caloric value.

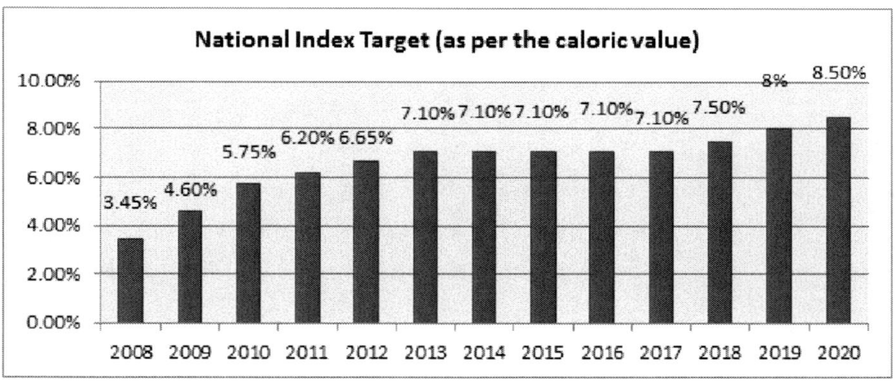


Source: *Act on biocomponents and liquid biofuels of 25 August 2006* (*Journal of Laws No. 169* item 1199, as amended), Regulation of the Council of Ministers of 13 August 2013 on National Index Targets for 2013-2018 *(Journal of Laws of 2013*, item 918), President of ARR's ordinance no. 173/2011/Z of 27 December 2011.

Figure 17. National Index Target (Narodowy Cel Wskaźnikowy, NCW) per a caloric value) in accordance with the regulation of the Council of Ministers.

Every entrepreneur conducting their business activity in the area of manufacturing, importing, or purchasing liquid fuels or liquid biofuels in the Community and selling or purchasing such fuels in a different form in the territory of the Republic of Poland or uses them for own purposes

(Article 2, section 1, point 25 of the act on biocomponents and liquid biofuels) is obliged to conform to the National Index Target (Figure 17).

In case of entities conforming to the National Index Target (e.g., PKN Orlen, Grupa Lotos), which have documented the annual use of at least 70% of biocomponents produced by manufacturers conducting business activity in the area of manufacturing biocomponents in the territory of EU, the minimum share, starting from 2012, is equal to the result of the multiplication of the reduction factor and the National Index Target.

In accordance with the ARR (Agencja Rynku Rolnego, Agricultural Market Agency) President's ordinance, a "manufacturer" is an entrepreneur conducting in the territory of the Republic of Poland a business activity in the area of manufacturing and storing biocomponents manufactured in Poland or placing them on the market. The reduction factor in 2012-2016 amounted to 0.85x. It allowed to achieve NCW of 6.03%. A current version of the project by the Council of Ministers includes a change of a reduction factor to the value of 0.82x. With such an assumption, it will be possible to achieve NCW of 6.396%. It may result in an increased demand for biocomponents. Orlen provisionally estimates that the NCW reduction factor proposed in the project of the ordinance would cause an increase of demand for esters in the scale of the country by ca. 85,000 tonnes.[153]

## 3.1.5. Legal Changes Related to Company Operations in Poland

### *3.1.5.1. Double Counting Principle*

The share of biocomponents manufactured from waste, remains, unused cellulose and lignocellulose material, counted according to its caloric value, is deemed doubled in the general amount of liquid fuels and biofuels sold off or marketed in other form in the territory of the Republic

---

[153] Based on www.nafta.wn.pl, access: 20 March, 2017.

of Poland by an entity conforming to the National Index Target or used by this entity for its own purposes in its territory[154].

### *3.1.5.2. In Case of Entities Confirming To NCW, the Rule Of 60% of Methyl Esters And 40% of B100*

It includes the minimum share of esters to entities conforming to NCW, which may mean greater need for ethyl esters of higher fatty acids.

### *3.1.5.3. Changes in the Energy Law*

They mostly include the introduction of requirement for the security on property for the companies operating in the area of fuels, in the form of owned assets or bank guarantee documenting the security.

Changes in regulations will not affect the current situation of the company. Alternatively, the need for biocomponents, including methyl esters, may increase, resulting in possible improvement of the company position on the market.

### *3.1.5.4. National Reduction Target (Narodowy Cel Redukcyjny, NCR)*

$CO_2$ emission reduction. The National Index Target and double counting will affect the way the biofuel market is shaped. Apart from these values, also National Reduction Targets (NCRs) resulting from a climate package will be stressed.

Companies executing NCR will ensure at least a minimum value of the reduction of greenhouse gases emission in fuel lifecycle. NCR will mean the obligation to reduce greenhouse gases by 4% till 2017 and by 6% till 2020 as compared to the level from 2010.[155] Thus, an important factor is the number of the manufacturers of biocomponents and liquid biofuels in Poland (Table 16).

---

[154] Based on the Act on biocomponents and liquid biofuels of 25 August 2006 (Dz. U. [Journal of Laws] of 2006 No. 169 item 1199).

[155] http://www.teraz-srodowisko.pl/aktualnosci/Szykuje-sie-rozwoj-biopaliw-wyzszej-generacji-1790.html, access: 24 November, 2016.

## Table 16. Characteristics of the biggest installations for the production of biocomponents and liquid biofuels in Poland

| No. | Name of manufacturer | The scope of operations | The type of installations | Installation annual productivity [millions of l] |
|---|---|---|---|---|
| 1 | EUROSERVICE Zakłady Przemysłu Tłuszczowego w Surochowie Sp. z o.o. | Manufacturing methyl esters | Installation to manufacture methyl esters | 272 |
| 2 | BIOAGRA-OIL S.A. | Manufacturing methyl esters | Ester production plant | 226 |
| 3 | WRATISLAVIA-BIO Sp. z o.o. | Manufacturing methyl esters | Installation to manufacture methyl esters | 170.09 |
| 4 | ORLEN POŁUDNIE S.A. | Manufacturing methyl esters | Installation to manufacture methyl esters | 170 |
| 5 | ADM MALBORK S.A. | Manufacturing methyl esters | Installation to manufacture methyl esters | 159 |
| 6 | DESTYLACJE POLSKIE Sp. z o.o. | Manufacturing bioethanol | No data | 150 |
| 7 | BIOAGRA S.A. | Manufacturing bioethanol | Molecular sieve | 150 |
| 8 | LOTOS BIOPALIWA Sp. z o.o. | Manufacturing methyl esters | Installation to manufacture methyl esters | 124.58 |
| 9 | AKWAWIT-POLMOS S.A. | Manufacturing bioethanol | Installation to manufacture bioethanol | 95 |
| 10 | ABTRANS Sp. z o.o. | Manufacturing methyl esters | Hydrodynamic and cavitation installation | 80 |

Source: A. Piwowar. 2015. Produkcja biokomponentów i biopaliw ciekłych w Polsce – tendencje rozwoju i regionalne zróżnicowanie. (In:) *Roczniki Naukowe Stowarzyszenia Ekonomistów Rolnictwa i Agrobiznesu XVII*, volume 2. Warszawa: 199.

## 3.2. Reasons for the Necessity of Restructuring

The company owner made the decision about performing the restructuring process in 2011. They decided to change the company management board in order to conduct restructuring. It shall be added that the company was founded in 2005. For its operations at that time, the company built an advanced technological line for the production of biocomponents, partially using external financing for that purpose. The aim was to perform a recovery restructuring and then, in the following years, to continue developing by winning customers and striving for the maximum usage of production lines. The achieved margin was supposed to cover the costs of company current operations, but also allow the company to pay back the amounts previously obtained as external financing for the construction of production lines.

In 2010, the company was in a difficult situation with most of its potential unused. As a result, the company decided that its restructuring was necessary in order to save its business from bankruptcy and winding up.

The financial situation of the company was very hard. At the beginning of 2011, the company did not operate, had no signed contracts, nor the capital necessary to introduce necessary changes.

### 3.2.1. Company Financial Situation before Restructuring

The elements of the financial analysis were used to evaluate the situation of Wratislavia Bio Sp. z o.o. The company financial reports were analyzed to assess its situation. Based on this data, the ratio analysis was used to evaluate the company situation in the period of 2008–2010.

First, the analysis of balance sheet of the company in 2008–2010 was performed (Table 17).

The analysis of the balance sheet shows the decrease in value of fixed assets in 2008–2010, and a significant downfall of current assets to the minimum level (Figure 18).

**Table 17. Wratislavia Bio Sp. z o.o.'s balance sheet for 2008–2010 (thousands of PLN)**

| ASSETS | 2008 | 2009 | 2010 |
|---|---|---|---|
| A. FIXED ASSETS | **94 858.80** | **87 598.30** | **77 731.90** |
| I INTANGIBLE ASSETS | 485.50 | 369.00 | 252.50 |
| II TANGIBLE FIXED ASSETS | 94 373.30 | 86 679.80 | 77 479.40 |
| III LONG-TERM RECEIVABLES | | | |
| IV LONG-TERM INVESTMENTS | | | |
| V LONG-TERM PREPAYMENTS | | 549.50 | |
| B. CURRENT ASSETS | **57 161.20** | **39 536.40** | **3 531.00** |
| I INVENTORY | 44 503.10 | 8 670.30 | 2 262.50 |
| II SHORT-TIME RECEIVABLES | 12 470.50 | 23 253.20 | 737.40 |
| III SHORT-TERM INVESTMENTS | 159.80 | 7 580.90 | 492.60 |
| IV SHORT-TERM PREPAYMENTS | 27.80 | 32.00 | 38.50 |
| TOTAL ASSETS | **152 020.00** | **127 134.70** | **81 262.90** |
| **LIABILITIES** | **2008** | **2009** | **2010** |
| A. EQUITY | 1 207.00 | 27 029.40 | 25 203.00 |
| B. LIABILITIES AND PROVISIONS FOR LIABILITIES | 150 813.00 | 100 105.20 | 56 059.90 |
| I PROVISIONS FOR LIABILITIES | 4 018.50 | 1 050.00 | 1 364.30 |
| II LONG-TERM LIABILITIES | 56 925.50 | 45 525.50 | 34 125.50 |
| III SHORT-TERM LIABILITIES | 89 598.40 | 53 529.70 | 20 570.10 |
| IV ACCRUALS | 270.60 | | |
| **TOTAL LIABILITIES** | **152 020.00** | **127 134.60** | **81 262.90** |

Source: Wratislavia Bio Sp. z o.o.'s financial data.

The analysis of liabilities shows the increase of equity in 2009 and 2010, but the value of liabilities and reserves significantly drops and reaches the level of PLN 56.06M in 2010 (Figure 19).

The balance sheet subject to a precise initial analysis including both horizontal and vertical analysis (Table 18). In the structure of assets, fixed assets significantly increased in 2008–2010. In 2008, fixed assets constituted 62% of all assets, and in 2010—already 96%. With regard to their value, however fixed assets decreased. Thus, in 2010 current assets constituted only 4%.

The share of equity increased and reached the level of 31% liabilities. The share of foreign capital decreased and amounted to 69%. With regard to its value, equity reached the highest value in 2009, and the lowest one the year before.

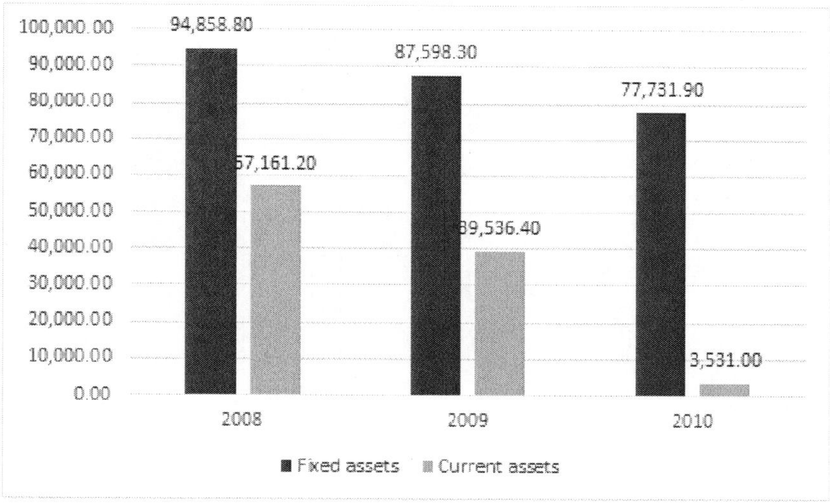


Source: Wratislavia Bio Sp. z o.o.'s financial data.

Figure 18. Fixed and current assets in Wratislavia Bio Sp. z. o.o. in 2008–2010 (thousands of PLN).

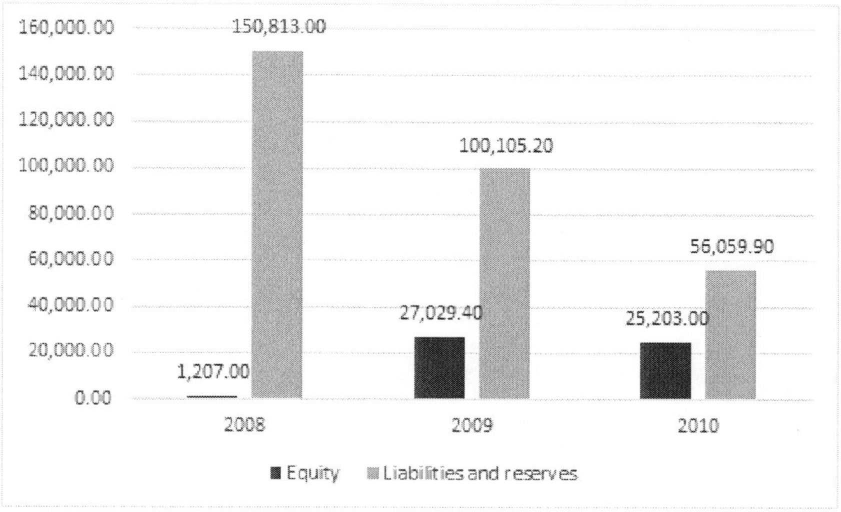


Source: Wratislavia Bio Sp. z o.o.'s financial data.

Figure 19. Equity and liabilities and reserves in Wratislavia Bio Sp. z. o.o. in 2008–2010 (thousands of PLN).

**Table 18. Horizontal and vertical analysis of Wratislavia Bio Sp z o.o.'s balance sheet**

| **Positions of the balance sheet/year** | **2008** | | **2009** | | | | **ROK 2010** | | | |
|---|---|---|---|---|---|---|---|---|---|---|
| ASSETS | Value (in thousands of PLN) | Structure in 2008 | Value (in thousands of PLN) | Dynamics in 2009/2008 | Rate of changes in 2009/2008 | Structure in 2009 | Value (in thousands of PLN) | Dynamics in 2010/2009 | Rate of changes in 2010/2009 | Structure in 2010 |
| **A. FIXED ASSETS** | **94 858.80** | **0.62** | **87 598.30** | **0.92** | **-0.08** | **0.69** | **77 731.90** | **0.89** | **-0.11** | **0.96** |
| I INTANGIBLE ASSETS | 485.50 | 0.01 | 369.00 | 0.76 | -0.24 | **0.00** | 252.50 | 0.68 | **-0.32** | 0.13 |
| II TANGIBLE FIXED ASSETS | 94 373.30 | 0.99 | 86 679.80 | 0.92 | -0.08 | **0.99** | 77 479.40 | 0.89 | **-0.11** | 1.00 |
| III LONG-TERM RECEIVABLES | | | | | | | | | **-1.00** | |
| IV LONG-TERM INVESTMENTS | | | | | | | | | **-1.00** | |
| V LONG-TERM PREPAYMENTS | | | 549.50 | | | **0.01** | | 0.00 | **-1.00** | |
| **B. CURRENT ASSETS** | **57 161.20** | **0.38** | **39 536.40** | **0.69** | **-0.31** | **0.31** | **3 531.00** | **0.09** | **-0.91** | **0.04** |
| I INVENTORY | 44 503.10 | 0.78 | 8 670.30 | 0.19 | -0.81 | 0.22 | 2 262.50 | 0.26 | **-0.74** | 0.64 |
| II SHORT-TIME RECEIVABLES | 12 470.50 | 0.22 | 23 253.20 | 1.86 | 0.86 | 0.59 | 737.40 | 0.03 | **-0.97** | 0.21 |
| III SHORT-TERM INVESTMENTS | 159.80 | 0.00 | 7 580.90 | 47.44 | 46.44 | 0.19 | 492.60 | 0.06 | **-0.94** | 0.14 |
| IV SHORT-TERM PREPAYMENTS | 27.80 | 0.00 | 32.00 | 1.15 | 0.15 | 0.00 | 38.50 | 1.20 | **0.20** | 0.01 |
| **TOTAL ASSETS** | **152 020.00** | **1.00** | **127 134.70** | **0.84** | **-0.16** | **1.00** | **81 262.90** | **0.64** | **-0.36** | |

| **Positions of the balance sheet/year** | **2008** | | **2009** | | | | **ROK 2010** | | | |
|---|---|---|---|---|---|---|---|---|---|---|
| **ASSETS** | Value (in thousands of PLN) | Structure in 2008 | Value (in thousands of PLN) | Dynamics in 2009/2008 | Rate of changes in 2009/2008 | Structure in 2009 | Value (in thousands of PLN) | Dynamics in 2010/2009 | Rate of changes in 2010/2009 | Structure in 2010 |
| **LIABILITIES** | **2008** | | **2009** | | | | **2010** | | **-1.00** | |
| A. EQUITY | 1 207.00 | 0.01 | 27 029.40 | 22.39 | 21.39 | **0.21** | 25 203.00 | 0.93 | **-0.07** | 0.31 |
| B. LIABILITIES AND PROVISIONS FOR LIABILITIES | 150 813.00 | 0.99 | 100 105.20 | 0.66 | -0.34 | **0.79** | 56 059.90 | 0.56 | **-0.44** | 0.69 |
| I PROVISIONS FOR LIABILITIES | 4 018.50 | 0.03 | 1 050.00 | 0.26 | -0.74 | 0.01 | 1 364.30 | 1.30 | **0.30** | 0.02 |
| II LONG-TERM LIABILITIES | 56 925.50 | 0.38 | 45 525.50 | 0.80 | -0.20 | 43.36 | 34 125.50 | 0.75 | **-0.25** | 0.61 |
| III SHORT-TERM LIABILITIES | 89 598.40 | 0.59 | 53 529.70 | 0.60 | -0.40 | 1.18 | 20 570.10 | 0.38 | **-0.62** | 0.37 |
| IV ACCRUALS | 270.60 | 0.00 | | | -1.00 | 0.00 | | | **-1.00** | |
| **TOTAL LIABILITIES** | **152 020.00** | **1.00** | **127 134.60** | **0.84** | **-0.16** | **1.00** | **81 262.90** | **0.64** | **-0.36** | **1.00** |

Source: Author's own analysis based on Wratislavia Bio Sp. z o.o.'s financial data.

**Table 19. Profit and loss account in Wratislavia Bio Sp. z. o.o. in 2008–2010 (thousands of PLN)**

| Profit and loss account | 2008 | 2009 | 2010 |
|---|---|---|---|
| **1. Base business** | | | |
| Net revenues from sales and equivalent | 183 076.20 | 305 661.50 | 77 337.30 |
| Internal cost of sales | 193 697.80 | 297 076.70 | 94 029.50 |
| **Result on sales** | **-10 621.60** | **8 584.80** | **-16 692.20** |
| **2. Other operating activities** | | | |
| Other operating revenues | 299.60 | 3 266.00 | 1 654.50 |
| Other operating expenses | 4 764.10 | 1 083.50 | 555.20 |
| **3. Operating result** | -15 086,10 | 10 767,30 | -15 592.90 |
| **4. Financial activities** | | | |
| Financial revenues | 106.90 | 94.20 | 35.20 |
| Financial expenses | 9 895.70 | 7 591.00 | 5 258.60 |
| **5. Extraordinary events** | | | |
| Result on extraordinary events | 0.00 | 0.00 | 0.00 |
| **6. Gross profit (loss)** | **-24 874.90** | **3 270.50** | **-20 816.30** |
| Income tax | -55.80 | -551.90 | 550.10 |
| **Net profit (loss)** | **-24 819.10** | **3 822.40** | **-21 366.40** |

Source: Wratislavia Bio Sp. z o.o.'s financial data.

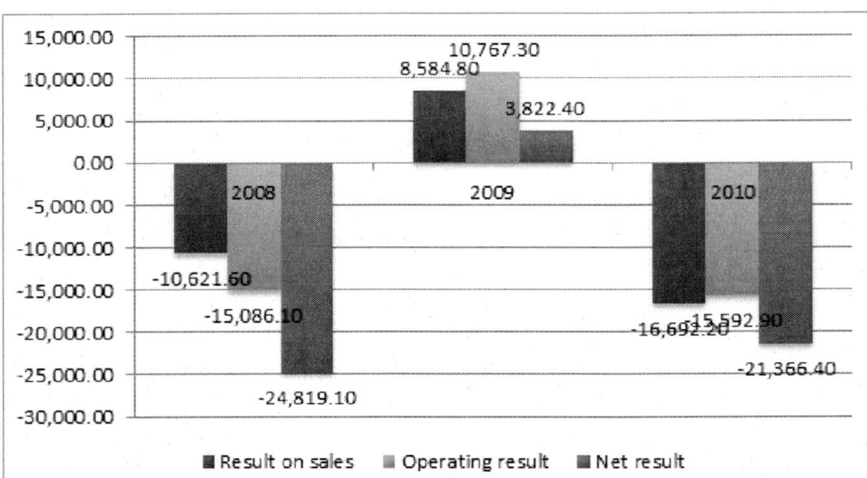


Source: Wratislavia Bio Sp. z o.o.'s financial data.

Figure 20. Result on sales, operating result, and net result in Wratislavia Bio Sp. z. o.o. in 2008–2010 (thousands of PLN).

The continued analysis of financial documents included the profit and loss account in the period of 2008-2010 (Table 19).

In 2008, there was an increase of net revenues. In 2009, the company presented a positive result on sales, operating results, and a positive net result. In 2010, the company experienced significant difficulties, because net revenues dramatically dropped, and the operating result and net result were negative (Figure 20).

The following element was an analysis of a cash flow statement in 2010 (Table 20).

**Table 20. Cash flow statement in Wratislavia Bio Sp. z o.o in 2010 (thousands of PLN)**

| No. | Change: | 2010 |
|---|---|---|
| I | Net cash flows from operating activities | -7 279.00 |
| II | Net cash flows from investment activities | -30 519.00 |
| III | Net cash flows from financial activities | 221 180.00 |
| IV | Total net cash flows (I+/-II+/-III) | 183 382.00 |

Source: Wratislavia Bio Sp. z o.o.'s financial data.

**Table 21. The analysis of cash flow in the company, taking the excess and deficiencies from specific areas of business (operating, investment, and financial activities) into consideration**

| | **Cases** | | | | | | | |
|---|---|---|---|---|---|---|---|---|
| **Stream type** | 1 | 2 | 3 | 4 | 5 | 6 | 7 | 8 |
| **Phase type** | A mature phrase | | | | A transitory phrase | | The phase of threat | |
| **Operating** | + | + | + | + | - | - | - | - |
| **Investment** | + | - | + | - | + | - | + | - |
| **Financial** | + | - | - | + | + | + | - | - |

Source: D. Wędzki. 2010. Wykorzystanie rachunku przepływów pieniężnych do analizy finansowej, "Rachunkowość", no. 1; E. Mioduchowska-Jaroszewicz. 2012. Ocena przepływów pieniężnych w grupach kapitałowych, Zeszyty Naukowe Uniwersytetu Szczecińskiego. Finanse. Rynki finansowe. Ubezpieczenia 56, 155-171.

The analysis of the cash flow account was performed with the use of information from literature pertaining to interpretation of cases and strategies related to the excess or deficiency of cash, based on the evaluation of the cash flow statement (Table 21).

These cases find their reflection in the company specific strategy[156] :

- Case 1: Positive cash flow on all levels. The company collects cash on its account in order to spend it, possibly, on future investments.
- Case 2: High return; profits are spent on the company's growth and liabilities.
- Case 3: A situation which often occurs during restructuring works.
- Case 4: A situation which is typical for a properly developing company.
- Case 5: Negative cash flow from operating activities and positive ones from other activities indicate that a company experiences temporary difficulties.
- Case 6: A situation which is typical for new and developing companies which have not reached their break-even and invest a lot.
- Case 7: Company cash shortages are covered with money from asset sale. It may mean that a company is in its last phase before going bankrupt.
- Case 8: Negative cash flow on all level, which, however, does not have to mean a bankruptcy. Such a company invests in spite of losing money and having to pay its earlier liabilities.

Based on the analysis, the situation of Wratislavia Bio Sp. z o.o. can be seen as case 6 to the transitory phase (Table 22), but other financial data indicate that the company is in a very difficult financial situation.

---

[156] E. Śnieżek. 2008. *Jak korzystać z rachunku przepływów pieniężnych*, Rachunkowość, no. 1, 21.

### 3.2.2. The Analysis of the Company's Situation before Restructuring

The company's situation was evaluated based on the ratio analysis including the following groups of ratios:

- Liquidity ratios,
- Debt ratios,
- Activity ratios,
- Profitability ratios.

### 3.2.3. Liquidity Analysis

Financial liquidity should be connected with the level of means of payment owned by the company, its ability to cover current liabilities and the possibility to turn property components into cash. Liquidity should be supervised by managing inflows and expenses. The value of inflows should be on the level which guarantees the possibility to pay back liabilities, and when inflows are too low, additional financing should be obtained[157]. It can be stressed that the value of company achieved net profit does not guarantee that the company has cash to settle its liabilities[158].

A basic measure evaluating the company's ability to repay its current liabilities in full by liquidating its current assets is the current liquidity ratio. It shows the relation of company current assets to its current liabilities. Its optimum value should be within 1.5-2[159].

$$\textbf{Current ratio} = \frac{\text{Current assets}}{\text{Short-term liabilities}} \tag{1}$$

[157] A. Ćwiąkała-Małys, W. Nowak. 2005. *Zarys metodologiczny analizy finansowej*. Wrocław: Uniwersytet Wrocławski: 105.

[158] W. Gabrusiewicz. 2002. *Podstawy analizy finansowej* Warszawa: PWE: 228.

[159] L. Bednarski. 2000. *Analiza finansowa w przedsiębiorstwie*. Warszawa: PWE: 78-79.

The current ratio (1) in Wratislavia-Bio Sp. z o. o. in 2008–2010 was at a very low level. In 2008, it amounted to 0.64, and then, it slightly improved in 2009 to the level of 0.74, reaching the lowest level in 2010, with its value of 0.17 (Table 22).

**Table 22. Current liquidity ratio in Wratislavia-Bio in 2008-2010**

| Ratio name | 2008 | 2009 | 2010 | Norm[160] |
|---|---|---|---|---|
| **Current ratio** | 0.64 | 0.74 | 0.17 | 1.2–2.0 |

Source: Author's own analysis based on Wratislavia Bio Sp. z o.o.'s financial data.

Next, a quick ratio (2), which shows the possibility to regularly repay short-term liabilities, was calculated.

$$\textbf{Quick ratio} = \frac{\text{Current assets} - \text{Inventories} - \text{Prepayments}}{\text{Short-term liabilities}} \tag{2}$$

The quick ratio in 2008–2010 amounted to, respectively, 0.14, 0.58, and 0.06 (Table 23). Thus, in the last year, its value was the lowest and the weakest in all analysed periods. The ratio level is significantly below the norm.

**Table 23. Quick ratio in Wratislavia-Bio in 2008-2010**

| Ratio name | 2008 | 2009 | 2010 | Norm |
|---|---|---|---|---|
| **Quick ratio** | 0.14 | 0.58 | 0.06 | 1-1.2 |

Source: Author's own analysis based on Wratislavia Bio Sp. z o.o.'s financial data.

In the liquidity analysis, the last analysed ratio was the cash to debt ratio (3).

160 The source of all norms is: M. Sierpińska, T. Jachna. 2004. *Ocena przedsiębiorstwa wg. standardów światowych*. Warszawa: PWN.

$$\textbf{Cash to debt ratio} = \frac{\text{Short-term investments}}{\text{Short-term liabilities}} \tag{3}$$

This ratio shows the value of current liabilities which a company should cover with its means of payment, but it does not determine company's solvability. The cash to debt ratio is thus a sign regarding the company's ability to pay[161]. It should be added that the higher the value of this ratio, the better the company ability to quickly pay back its current liabilities. If this ratio is too high, it may mean that cash is used ineffectively in a company. In the cash to debt ratio (Table 24), the calculations include the value of short-term investments instead of only their part in the form of cash, due to the availability of financial data.

**Table 24. Cash to debt ratio in Wratislavia-Bio in 2008-2010**

| **Ratio name** | 2008 | 2009 | 2010 | Norm |
|---|---|---|---|---|
| **Cash to debt ratio** | 0.0018 | 0.1416 | 0.0239 | No standard in practice |

Source: Author's own analysis based on Wratislavia Bio Sp. z o.o.'s financial data.

### 3.2.4. Liquidity Analysis — A Summary

The cash to debt ratio was on the normative level only in 2009. In the remaining part of the studied period, the value of this ratio was definitely below the required level.

Concentrating on financial liquidity (Figure 20), we should indicate and emphasize without a doubt that the Company has significant problems with liquidity. Almost all ratios are definitely below the required, normative level. This shows that the company was in a very difficult situation and had problems with settling its liabilities.

---

[161] L. Bednarski. 2000. *Analiza finansowa w przedsiębiorstwie*. Warszawa: Wyd. PWE: 80.

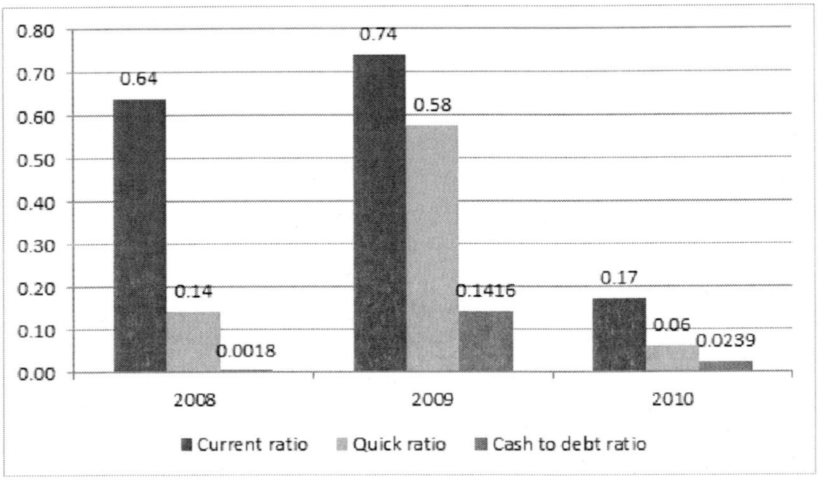


Source: Author's own analysis based on Wratislavia Bio Sp. z o.o.'s financial data.

Figure 20. Graphic representation of liquidity ratios in Wratislavia-Bio Sp. z o. o.

### *3.2.4.1. Debt Analysis*

The analysis of the debt level allows to evaluate the company and its financial independency and capability to repay liabilities on time[162]. For the analysis, four debt ratios have been selected, leading to the conclusions.

The first ratio to be calculated was debt ratio (4).

$$\textbf{Debt ratio} = \frac{\text{Total debts}}{\text{Total assets}} \tag{4}$$

Debt ratio (Table 25) reached the highest level of 0.96 in 2008. In the following years, the level of this ratio decreased and reached 0.67 in 2010. This means that there was a significant debt, but it was gradually reduced.

**Table 25. Debt ratio in Wratislavia-Bio in 2008-2010**

| **Ratio name** | 2008 | 2009 | 2010 | Norm |
|---|---|---|---|---|
| **Debt ratio** | 0.96 | 0.78 | 0.67 | 0.57-0.67 |

Source: Author's own analysis based on Wratislavia Bio Sp. z o.o.'s financial data.

162 K. Marecki. 2002. *Rachunkowość menedżerska w gospodarce finansowej przedsiębiorstwa.* 2nd ed. Warszawa: Difin: 195.

The second ratio (5) which was included in the debt analysis was debt to equity ratio, which is an information about the relation between total company's liabilities to its equity[163]. The increase of this ratio leads to the growth of risk for lenders and shareholders[164].

$$\textbf{Debt to equity ratio} = \frac{\text{Total liabilities}}{\text{Equity}} \tag{5}$$

The highest value of the company debt to equity ratio (Table 26) was reported in 2008. Then, it gradually dropped, reaching 2.17 in 2010.

**Table 26. Debt to equity ratio in Wratislavia-Bio in 2008-2010**

| **Ratio name** | 2008 | 2009 | 2010 | Norm |
|---|---|---|---|---|
| **Debt to equity ratio** | 121.40 | 3.66 | 2.17 | 0.75 |

Source: Author's own analysis based on Wratislavia Bio Sp. z o.o.'s financial data.

The next ratio considered in the analysis of the company debt is a long-term debt to equity ratio (6).

$$\textbf{Long term debt to equity} = \frac{\text{Long-term liabilities}}{\text{Equity}} \tag{6}$$

The value of the debt to equity ratio was too high (Table 27), which means that long-term liabilities significantly exceeded owned equity.

**Table 27. Long-term debt to equity in Wratislavia-Bio in 2008-2010**

| **Ratio name** | 2008 | 2009 | 2010 | Norm |
|---|---|---|---|---|
| **Long term debt to equity** | 47.16 | 47.54 | 1.68 | 0.5-1 |

Source: Author's own analysis based on Wratislavia Bio Sp. z o.o.'s financial data.

---

[163] K. Sawicki, ed. 2001. *Polityka bilansowa i analiza finansowa. Nowoczesne instrumenty zarządzania firmą.* Wrocław: Wyd. Ekspert: 138.

[164] K. Marecki. 2002. *Rachunkowość menedżerska w gospodarce finansowej przedsiębiorstwa.* 2nd ed. Warszawa: Difin: 196.

The last ratio included in the indebtness ratios is the fixed assets debt ratio (7). It informs about the security of liabilities with fixed assets. This ratio is important from the perspective of lenders, because credits are usually secured with fixed assets.

$$\textbf{Fixed assets debt ratio} = \frac{\text{Tangible current assets}}{\text{Long-term liabilities}} \quad (7)$$

The fixed assets debt ratio tended to increase (Table 28). In 2008-2010, it amounted to, respectively, 1.66, 1.90, and 2.27. The value of fixed assets increased as compared to long-term liabilities.

**Table 28. Fixed assets debt ratio in Wratislavia-Bio in 2008-2010**

| **Ratio name** | 2008 | 2009 | 2010 | Norm |
|---|---|---|---|---|
| **Fixed assets debt** | 1.66 | 1.90 | 2.27 | |

Source: Author's own analysis based on Wratislavia Bio Sp. z o.o.'s financial data.

## 3.2.5. Debt Analysis — A Summary

The analysis of debt shows the excessive debt of the company, whose operations, as a result, are under a great risk. Due to an extremely high debt ratio, the company was in danger of insolvency, but in two years that followed, its debt ratio significantly decreased. The debt to equity ratio was also high, and, during two years, it dropped to the level which was still quite high and could pose a threat to the company's operations in the future. Long-term liabilities were significantly higher than owned equity, which caused a high level of long-term debt to equity in 2010 (2.27).

### *3.2.5.1. Activity Efficiency Analysis*

The analysis with the use of different types of ratios presents the level of efficient use of assets and capital.

First, the asset turnover ratio (8) was calculated.

$$\textbf{Asset turnover ratio} = \frac{\text{Net revenues from sale}}{\text{Total assets}} \quad (8)$$

It informs about the efficiency of using assets by the company. It is assumed that entities which have a relatively low profit margin present a high ratio of turnover and assets, and the companies with a relatively high margin have a comparably low asset turnover ratio[165].

In 2008-2010, the asset turnover ratio in Wratislavia-Bio significantly fluctuated (Table 29). In 2009, the value of this ratio amounted to as high as 2.4, while in the following year, it dropped to 0.95.

**Table 29. Asset turnover ratio in Wratislavia-Bio in 2008-2010**

| **Ratio name** | 2008 | 2009 | 2010 | Norm |
|---|---|---|---|---|
| **Asset turnover ratios** | 1.20 | 2.40 | 0.95 | The higher, the better |

Source: Author's own analysis based on Wratislavia Bio Sp. z o.o.'s financial data.

After analyzing the asset turnover ratio, the study focused on calculations of ratios related to receivables. The receivables turnover ratio (9) was calculated to indicate the number of turnover cycles.

$$\textbf{Receivables turnover ratio} = \frac{\text{Net revenues from sale}}{\text{Total receivables}} \quad (9)$$

In 2008 and 2009, this ratio was stable (Table 30). It significantly increased in 2010, which should indicate that the company's situation company improved, but in the case of a company which stopped manufacturing and selling, the value of this ratio can be negatively interpreted. The lack of sale leads to the decrease of receivables and results in extremely high value of the receivables turnover ratio. This is also reflected in the value of revenues, which in 2010 were definitely lower than in the previous periods.

To complement the receivables turnover ratio, the days sales outstanding was also calculated (10).

---

[165] G. Gołębiowski, A. Tłaczała. 2009. *Analiza finansowa w teorii i w praktyce*. Warszawa: Difin: 198.

$$\textbf{Days sales outstanding} = \frac{\text{Total receivables}*360}{\text{Net revenues from sale}} \tag{10}$$

The days sales outstanding (Table 31) had a similar value in 2008–2009 – it increased from 24.52 to 27.39. It is worth emphasizing, however, that in the following year it reached the level of 3.43. In normal conditions of company functioning, this would mean an improvement of the situation. However, in this case, due to stopped manufacturing and dropping sales, the value of receivables decreased significantly faster than the sales dropped. As a result, and in comparison to the receivables turnover ratio, it should be emphasized that receivables were paid quickly, because their amount was decreasing. This meant that the situation of Wratislavia-Bio was deteriorating.

**Table 30. Receivables turnover ratio in Wratislavia-Bio in 2008-2010**

| **Ratio name** | 2008 | 2009 | 2010 | Norm |
|---|---|---|---|---|
| **Receivables turnover ratio** | 14.68 | 13.14 | 104.88 | The higher the better |

Source: Author's own analysis based on Wratislavia Bio Sp. z o.o.'s financial data.

**Table 31. Days sales outstanding in Wratislavia-Bio in 2008-2010**

| **Ratio name** | 2008 | 2009 | 2010 | Norm |
|---|---|---|---|---|
| **Days sales outstanding** | 24.52 | 27.39 | 3.43 | The less, the better |

Source: Author's own analysis based on Wratislavia Bio Sp. z o.o.'s financial data.

Then, the ratios related to inventory, starting from the inventory turnov ratio, were calculated (11).

$$\textbf{Inventory turnover ratio} = \frac{Net\ revenues\ from\ sale}{Inventory} \tag{11}$$

Inventory turnover (Table 32) had dynamically increased since 2009 and reached the value of 35.25 in 2009, and 34.18 in 2010.

**Table 32. Inventory turnover ratio in Wratislavia-Bio in 2008-2010**

| Ratio name | 2008 | 2009 | 2010 | Norm |
|---|---|---|---|---|
| **Inventory turnover ratio** | 4.11 | 35.25 | 34.18 | The lower value, the bigger product turnover |

Source: Author's own analysis based on Wratislavia Bio Sp. z o.o.'s financial data.

In the analysis of inventory, the days inventory turnover ratio (12) was calculated to inform about the number of days when the inventory is not sold and stays in warehouses.

$$\textbf{Days inventory turnover ratio} = \frac{Inventory*360}{Net\ revenues\ from\ sale} \qquad (12)$$

The value of the days inventory turnover ratio decreased in 2009, and stayed on the same level, which exceeded 10 days (Table 33).

**Table 33. Days inventory turnover ratio in Wratislavia-Bio in 2008-2010**

| Ratio name | 2008 | 2009 | 2010 | Norm |
|---|---|---|---|---|
| **Days inventory turnover ratio** | 87.51 | 10.21 | 10.53 | The less, the better |

Source: Author's own analysis based on Wratislavia Bio Sp. z o.o.'s financial data.

The next ratio was related to the analysis of liabilities turnover (13).

$$\textbf{Days liabilities turnover ratio} = \frac{Short-term\ liabilities*360}{Net\ revenues\ from\ sale} \qquad (13)$$

The liabilities turnover ratio (Table 34) was the highest in 2008. Then, it significantly improved and reached the level of 63.05 in 2009. In the following year, it dramatically worsened and reached the value of 95.75. Liabilities were settled late, which showed that the company was in a difficult situation.

**Table 34. Days liabilities turnover ratio in Wratislavia-Bio in 2008-2010**

| Ratio name | 2008 | 2009 | 2010 | Norm |
|---|---|---|---|---|
| **Ratio of paying back liabilities in days** | 176.19 | 63.05 | 95.75 | The lower value, the better |

Source: Author's own analysis based on Wratislavia Bio Sp. z o.o.'s financial data.

While taking into consideration turnover ratios, the cash ratio was calculated (14).

- **Cash ratio** = days receivables turnover ratio + days cycle of inventory – days liabilities turnover ratio [14].

Cash ratio (Table 35) was negative, which means that, thanks to the sale of products, there was a quick return of assets invested in production.

**Table 35. Cash ratio in Wratislavia-Bio in 2008-2010**

| Ratio name | 2008 | 2009 | 2010 | Norm |
|---|---|---|---|---|
| **Cash ratio** | -64.15 | -25.45 | -81.79 | The lower value, the better |

Source: Author's own analysis based on Wratislavia Bio Sp. z o.o.'s financial data.

### 3.2.6. Activity Efficiency Analysis — A Summary

The turnover ratios (Table 36) for receivables decreased, but it was caused by the company's financial situation and its decreasing production and sales. The turnover ratios for liabilities varied, but the periods, in general, were long. The days inventory turnover ratio amounted to 10.53, which meant that there were no stock products in warehouses. Financing was possible due to taking on receivables, which, in 2008 – 2009, were covered after 176.19, 63.05, and 95.75 days.

**Table 36. Days turnover ratios in Wratislavia-Bio in 2008-2010**

| **Turnover in days** | | | |
|---|---|---|---|
| Ratio/Year | 2008 | 2009 | 2010 |
| Receivables | 24.52 | 27.39 | 3.43 |
| Inventory | 87.51 | 10.21 | 10.53 |
| Liabilities | 176.19 | 63.05 | 95.75 |

Source: Author's own analysis based on Wratislavia Bio Sp. z o.o.'s financial data.

Based on its cash cycle, the company was in a difficult situation, but 2010 was a beneficial year, because the company received payments from its customers a long time before it paid its liabilities.

### *3.2.6.1. Profitability Analysis*

Profitability ratios are a reflection of the relation between a financial result and turnover, or engaged resources. They function as a summary of the ratio analysis, and allow to determine company's earning capacity and define its source[166].

First, a ratio called ROS[167] (14), informing about the financial results achieved from sales, was calculated.

$$\textbf{Return on sales} = \frac{Net\ income}{Net\ revenues\ from\ sale} \qquad (14)$$

It was only in 2009 when the company did not suffer loss, and its return on sales was positive (Table 37).

**Table 37. Return on sales in Wratislavia-Bio in 2008-2010**

| **Ratio name** | 2008 | 2009 | 2010 | Norm |
|---|---|---|---|---|
| **Return on sales** | -0.14 | 0.01 | -0.28 | The higher the value, the better |

Source: Author's own analysis based on Wratislavia Bio Sp. z o.o.'s financial data.

---

166K. Sawicki, ed. 2001. *Polityka bilansowa i analiza finansowa. Nowoczesne instrumenty zarządzania firmą.* Wrocław: Wyd. Ekspert: 151-152.

167 Return on Sales.

The next used ratio was ROA[168] (15) informing how much profit was achieved from owned assets.

$$\textbf{Return on assets} = \frac{Net\ income}{Total\ assets} \qquad (15)$$

The asset profitability (Table 38), as in case of return on sales, was negative in 2008 and 2009.

**Table 38. Return on assets in Wratislavia-Bio in 2008-2010**

| Ratio name | 2008 | 2009 | 2010 | Norm |
|---|---|---|---|---|
| **Return on assets** | -0.16 | 0.03 | -0.26 | The higher the value, the better |

Source: Author's own analysis based on Wratislavia Bio Sp. z o.o.'s financial data.

The analysis also included one more ratio – ROE[169] (16).

$$\textbf{Return on equity} = \frac{Net\ income}{Equity} \qquad (16)$$

The return on equity (Table 39) was negative in 2008 and in 2010. Since the company made a profit in 2009, the ratio was positive for that year.

**Table 39. Return on equity in Wratislavia-Bio in 2008-2010**

| Ratio name | 2008 | 2009 | 2010 | Norm |
|---|---|---|---|---|
| **Return on equity** | -20.56 | 0.14 | -0.85 | The higher the value, the better |

Source: Author's own analysis based on Wratislavia Bio Sp. z o.o.'s financial data.

The last ratio included in the profitability analysis was return on investment – ROI (17).

$$\textbf{Return on investment} = \frac{Operating\ result}{Total\ assets} \qquad (17)$$

---

[168] Return on Assets.

[169] Return on Equity.

**Table 40. Return on investment in Wratislavia-Bio in 2008-2010**

| Ratio name | 2008 | 2009 | 2010 | Norm |
|---|---|---|---|---|
| **Return on investment** | -0.10 | 0.08 | -0.19 | The higher the value, the better |

Source: Author's own analysis based on Wratislavia Bio Sp. z o.o.'s financial data.

The return on investment (Table 40) complements return on equity (ROE) and return on assets (ROA). ROI includes an operating result in order to apply only to the company base activity. In the studied company, the result was positive only in 2009.

### 3.2.7. Profitability Analysis – A Summary

To sum up the analysis, profitability ratios (Figure 22) were on an acceptable level only in 2009. In the remaining years, due to the fact that the company suffered a net loss, these ratios were negative. It was necessary to handle this difficult financial situation and establish a strategy to limit or completely eliminate suffered net loss.

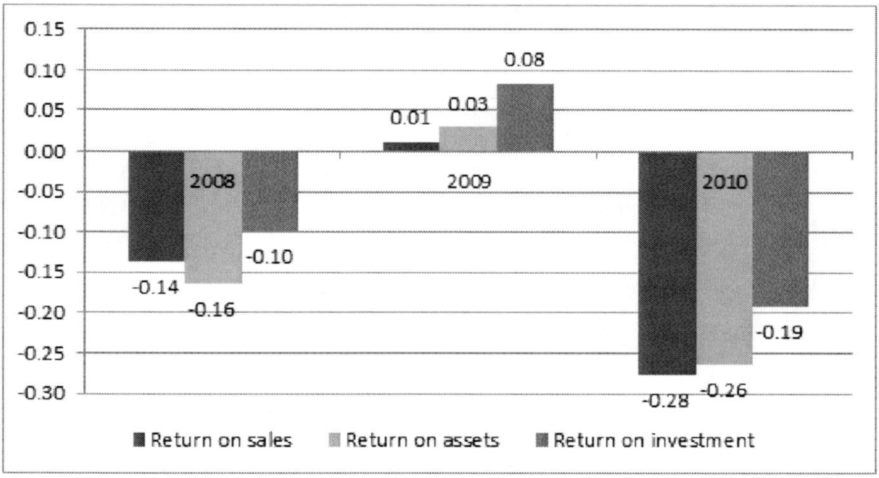


Source: Author's own analysis based on Wratislavia Bio Sp. z o.o.'s financial data.

Figure 22. Profitability ratios in Wratislavia-Bio in 2008-2010.

| NET RESULT | |
|---|---|
| **2008** | -24 819.10 |
| **2009** | 3 822.40 |
| **2010** | -21 366.40 |

/

| NET REVENUE FROM SALES | |
|---|---|
| **2008** | 183 076.20 |
| **2009** | 305 661.50 |
| **2010** | 77 337.30 |

=

| RETURN ON SALES | |
|---|---|
| 2008 | -13.56% |
| 2009 | 1.25% |
| 2010 | -27.63% |

x

| NET REVENUE FROM SALES | |
|---|---|
| **2008** | 183 076.20 |
| **2009** | 305 661.50 |
| **2010** | 77 337.30 |

/

| TOTAL ASSETS | |
|---|---|
| **2008** | 152 020.00 |
| **2009** | 127 134.60 |
| **2010** | 81 262.90 |

=

| ASSET TURNOVER | |
|---|---|
| 2008 | 1.20 |
| 2009 | 2.40 |
| 2010 | 0.95 |

=

| RETURN ON ASSETS | |
|---|---|
| 2008 | -0.16 |
| 2009 | 0.03 |
| 2010 | -0.26 |

x

| TOTAL ASSETS | |
|---|---|
| 2008 | 152 020.00 |
| 2009 | 127 134.60 |
| 2010 | 81 262.90 |

/

| EQUITY | |
|---|---|
| 2008 | 1 207.00 |
| 2009 | 27 029.40 |
| 2010 | 25 203.00 |

=

| MULTIPLIER OR EQUITY | |
|---|---|
| 2008 | 125.95 |
| 2009 | 4.70 |
| 2010 | 3.22 |

=

| RETURN ON EQUITY | |
|---|---|
| 2008 | -20.56 |
| 2009 | 0.14 |
| 2010 | -0.85 |

Source: Author's own analysis based on Wratislavia Bio Sp. z o.o.'s financial data.

Figure 23. DuPont model in 2008–2010 in Wratislavia-Bio Sp. z. o. o.

The profitability analysis was complemented with DuPont model (Figure 23), indicating company areas which require changes in order to improve return on equity. In the analysed case, the multiplier of equity should be affected by increasing return on sales and capital.

In the next step, the ratios supporting the above calculations were calculated to determine the company's net working capital (18).

$$\textbf{Net working capital (pl. KON)} = \text{Constant capital}^{170} - \text{fixed assets} \quad (18)$$

Net working capital (Table 41) was negative each year. In 2008, it amounted to PLN -36,730,000 and PLN -18,400,000 in 2010.

**Table 41. Net working capital in Wratislavia-Bio Sp. z. o. o. (in thousands of PLN)**

| **Ratio name** | 2008 | 2009 | 2010 |
|---|---|---|---|
| **Net working capital** | -36,726,30 | -15,043,40 | -18,403,40 |

Source: Author's own analysis based on Wratislavia Bio Sp. z o.o.'s financial data.

Apart from KON, two other ratios were calculated: a golden (19) and silver (20) rule of balance sheet.

$$\textbf{Golden rule of balance sheet} = \frac{Equity}{Fixed\ assets} \quad (19)$$

$$\textbf{Silver rule of balance sheet} = \frac{Constant\ capital}{Fixed\ assets} \quad (20)$$

The golden and silver rule of balance sheet are below 100% (Table 42), so, in financing fixed assets, they are supported not only by equity, but also by foreign capital. In 2010, the ratios amounted to, respectively, 32.42% and 76.32%.

---

[170] Constant capital = Equity + Long-term liabilities.

**Table 42. Golden and silver rule of balance sheet in Wratislavia-Bio Sp. z. o. o.**

| Ratio name | Calculation method | 2008 | 2009 | 2010 |
|---|---|---|---|---|
| Golden rule of balance sheet | (E/FA) x 100% | 1.27% | 30.86% | 32.42% |
| Silver rule of balance sheet | (CC/FA) x 100% | 61.28% | 82.83% | 76.32% |

Source: Author's own analysis based on Wratislavia Bio Sp. z o.o.'s financial data.

The following element in the evaluation of the company's financial situation was to calculate the Altman's model according to a modified model used for developing markets (21).

$$\textbf{EM score} = 6.56\,X1 + 3.26\,X2 + 6.72\,X3 + 1.05\,X4 + 3.35 \qquad (21)$$

where:

X1 – net working capital/assets;

X2 – accumulated retained earnings (total value of retained earnings from years preceding the study)/assets;

X3 – EBIT/assets;

X4 – equity market value/debt book value.

The results of EM score are interpreted in the following way:

- (0–5.5 > high risk of bankruptcy;
- (5.5–∞) low risk of bankruptcy.

**Table 43. Altman's model for developing markets in Wratislavia-Bio Sp. z. o. o.**

| Year | 2008 | 2009 | 2010 |
|---|---|---|---|
| **Altman's model for developing markets** | 0.4747 | 3.4274 | 0.1016 |

Source: Author's own analysis based on Wratislavia Bio Sp. z o.o.'s financial data.

The results of the Altman's model for developing markets indicated that in 2008–2010, there was a high risk of company's bankruptcy due to its difficult financial and property-related situation. The results of the model amounted to, respectively: 0.4747, 3.4274, and 0.1016 (Table 43). All values are definitely below the limit value of 5.5.

After the initial analysis and ratio analysis with additional ratios, the study concentrated on performance indicators.

**Table 44. Absolute accounting measures of efficiency in Wratislavia-Bio in 2008-2010**

| ACCOUNTING MEASURES OF EFFICIENCY | | | | | |
|---|---|---|---|---|---|
| Absolute measures (in thousands of PLN) | | | | | |
| EBIT | NP + INT + T | EBIT – Earnings Before Interest (Operating Profit) | 2008 | 2009 | 2010 |
| | | NP – Net Profit | -15 086.10 | 10 767.30 | -15 592.90 |
| | | INT – Interest | | | |
| | | T – Tax | | | |
| EBITDA | EBIT + DEP | EBITDA – Earnings Before Interest, Taxes, Depreciation, and Amortization | ND | 15 860.07 | -6 245.45 |
| | | EBIT – Earnings Before Interest (Operating Profit) | | | |
| | | DEP – Depreciation | | | |
| NOPAT | EBIT x (1 - T) | NOPAT – Net Operating Profit After Tax | -12 219.74 | 8 721.51 | -12 630.25 |
| | | EBIT – Earnings Before Interest (Operating Profit) | | | |
| | | T – Tax | | | |
| EBIDAAT | (EBIT + DEP) x (1 - T) | EBIDAAT – Earnings Before Interest, Depreciation and Amortization, After Taxes | | 12 846.65 | -5 058.82 |
| | | EBIT – Earnings Before Interest (Operating Profit) | | | |
| | | DEP – Depreciation | | | |
| | | T – Tax | | | |
| EPS | NP/number of shares | EPS – earnings per share | - | - | - |

Source: Author's own analysis based on Wratislavia Bio Sp. z o.o.'s financial data, and A. Jaki. 2013. *Pomiar i ocena efektywności kreowania wartości w przedsiębiorstwie.* Finanse, Rynki Finansowe, Ubezpieczenia no. 59 (760). Szczecin: 135.

### *3.2.7.1. Company Performance Indicators before Restructuring*

Wratislavia-Bio Sp. z. o.o.'s financial situation was evaluated with the use of absolute and relative measures grouped in the following categories:

- Accounting efficiency measures,
- Financial efficiency measures,
- Market efficiency measures.

First, the absolute accounting efficiency measures (Table 44) were calculated. The company's operating result required improvement and indicated the company difficult financial situation. EBITDA, NOPAT, and EBIDAAT were negative in 2009.

After calculating absolute measures, the relative accounting measures of efficiency were counted (Table 45). The most noticeable aspect is the negative value of profitability ratios and the high level of financial leverage amounting to 4.45 in 2010.

After calculating accounting measures of efficiency, the study included the calculation of financial measures of efficiency (Table 46). All absolute measures had negative values in 2010 which demonstrated a general lack of free cash flow. DCF and NPV were not calculated due to the lack of data. Also, in the studied period, the company did not make any investments.

The next group of ratios were relative financial measures of efficiency (Table 47). Among them, it was possible to show the value of weighted average cost of capital (WACC) which was calculated as a relation of financial costs to total liabilities, so it included only the cost of debt, which increased throughout the years.

Then, the analysis included market measures of efficiency (Table 48). Their calculation was possible thanks to the data availability and executed investments of an economic value added ratio (EVA$^{TM}$), which was negative and amounted to PLN -16,810,000 in 2010.

## Table 45. Relative accounting measures of efficiency in Wratislavia-Bio in 2008-2010

| | | | | | |
|---|---|---|---|---|---|
| **ACCOUNTING MEASURES OF EFFICIENCY** | | | | | |
| Relative measures | | | | | |
| ROI | NOPAT/K | ROI – Return on Invested Capital | 2008 | 2009 | 2010 |
| | | NOPAT – Net Operating Profit After Tax | -0.08 | 0.07 | -0.16 |
| | | K – total capital (with the sum of liabilities included) | | | |
| ROA | NP/A | ROA – net Return on Assets | -0.16 | 0.03 | -0.26 |
| | | NP – Net Profit | | | |
| | | A – total assets | | | |
| ROS | NP/S | ROS – Return on Sales | -0.14 | 0.01 | -0.28 |
| | | NP – Net Profit | | | |
| | | S – net sales | | | |
| ROE | NP/E | NP – Net Profit | -20.56 | 0.14 | -0.85 |
| | | E – Equity | | | |
| DFL | (ROE - ROI)/ROI | DFL – Degree of Financial Leverage | 254.81 | 1.06 | 4.45 |
| | | ROE – Return on Equity | | | |
| | | ROI – Return on Invested Capital | | | |
| DOL | (S - VC)/EBIT | DOL – Degree of Operational Leverage | 0.70 | 0.80 | 1.07 |
| | | S – net sales | | | |
| | | VC – Variable Costs | | | |

Source: Author's own analysis based on Wratislavia Bio Sp. z o.o.'s financial data, and A. Jaki. 2013. *Pomiar i ocena efektywności kreowania wartości w przedsiębiorstwie*. Finanse, Rynki Finansowe, Ubezpieczenia no. 59 (760). Szczecin: 135.

## Table 46. Absolute financial measures of efficiency in Wratislavia-Bio in 2008-2010

| | | | | | |
|---|---|---|---|---|---|
| **FINANCIAL MEASURES OF EFFICIENCY** | | | | | |
| Absolute measures (in thousands of PLN) | | | | | |
| FCF | NOPAT + DEP - I - ΔWC | FCF – Free Cash Flow | 2008 | 2009 | 2010 |
| | | NOPAT – Net Operating Profit After Tax | ND | 17 174.28 | -3 282.80 |
| | | DEP – Depreciation | | | |
| | | I – investment capital | | | |
| | | ΔWC – net change in working capital | | | |
| FCFE | NP + DEP – I -ΔWC + ΔD | FCFE – Free Cash Flow to Equity | ND | -129 349.62 | -3 282.80 |
| | | NP – Net Profit | | | |
| | | DEP – Depreciation | | | |
| | | I – investment capital | | | |
| | | ΔWC – net change in working capital | | | |
| | | ΔD – net increase in debt | | | |
| GCF | NOPAT + DEP | GCF – Gross Cash Flow | ND | 13 814.28 | -3 282.80 |
| | | NOPAT – Net Operating Profit After Tax | | | |
| | | DEP – Depreciation | | | |
| DCF | $CF \times 1/(1 + r)^n$ | DCF – Discounted Cash Flow | - | - | - |
| | | CF – Cash Flow | | | |
| | | r – discount rate | | | |
| | | n – number of years | | | |

| | | | | | |
|---|---|---|---|---|---|
| NPV | $\sum NCF \times 1/(1 + r)^n - \sum I\ 1/(1 + r)^n$ | NPV – Net Present Value | ND | ND | ND |
| | | NCF – Net Cash Flow | | | |
| | | r – discount rate | | | |
| | | n – number of years | | | |
| | | I – investment capital | | | |
| CVA | K x (CFROI - WACC) = GCF - K x WACC | CVA – Cash Value Added | ND | 8 915.17 | -12 018.95 |
| | | K – total capital | | | |
| | | CFROI – Cash Flow Return on Investment | | | |
| | | WACC – Weighted Average Cost of Capital | | | |
| | | GCF – Gross Cash Flow | | | |

Source: Author's own analysis based on Wratislavia Bio Sp. z o.o.'s financial data, and A. Jaki. 2013. *Pomiar i ocena efektywności kreowania wartości w przedsiębiorstwie*. Finanse, Rynki Finansowe, Ubezpieczenia no. 59 (760). Szczecin: 135.

## Table 47. Relative financial measures of efficiency in Wratislavia-Bio in 2008-2010

| | | | | | |
|---|---|---|---|---|---|
| **FINANCIAL MEASURES OF EFFICIENCY** | | | | | |
| Relative measures | | | | | |
| IRR | $\sum NCF \times 1/(1 + IRR)^n =$ | IRR – Internal Return Rate | 2008 | 2009 | 2010 |
| | $\sum I \times 1/(1 + IRR)^n$ | NCF – Net Cash Flow | ND | ND | ND |
| | | n – number of years | | | |
| CFROI | $\sum NCF \times 1/(1 + CFROI)^n =$ | CFROI – Cash Flow Return on Investment | ND | ND | ND |
| | $\sum I \times 1/(1 + CFROI)^n$ | NCF – Net Cash Flow | | | |
| | | n – number of years | | | |
| WACC | $k_e \times E/K + k_d \times D/K$ | WACC – Weighted Average Cost of Capital | 6.76% | 8.30% | 9.70% |
| | | ke – cost of equity | | | |
| | | kd – cost of foreign capital (debt) | | | |
| | | E – equity | | | |
| | | D – foreign capital (debt) | | | |
| | | K – total capital | | | |

Source: Author's own analysis based on Wratislavia Bio Sp. z o.o.'s financial data, and A. Jaki. 2013. *Pomiar i ocena efektywności kreowania wartości w przedsiębiorstwie*. Finanse, Rynki Finansowe, Ubezpieczenia no. 59 (760). Szczecin: 135.

## Table 48. Absolute market measures of efficiency in Wratislavia-Bio in 2008-2010

| MARKET MEASURES OF EFFICIENCY | | | | | |
|---|---|---|---|---|---|
| Absolute measures (in thousands of PLN) | | | | | |
| EVA™ | K x (ROI - WACC) = NOPAT - K x WACC | EVA™ – Economic Value Added | 2008 | 2009 | 2010 |
| | | K – total capital | -22 486.63 | 29 052.36 | -16 813.01 |
| | | ROI – Return on Invested capital | | | |
| | | WACC - Weighted Average Cost of Capital | | | |
| | | NOPAT – Net Operating Profit After Tax | | | |
| EVC | E x (ROE - $k_e$) = NP - E x $k_e$ | K – total capital | ND | ND | ND |
| | | ROI – Return on Invested capital | | | |
| | | WACC – Weighted Average Cost of Capital | | | |
| | | NOPAT – Net Operating Profit After Tax | | | |
| | | EVC – Estimated Value Created | | | |
| MVA | V(K) - K = V(E) - E | MVA – Market Value Added | ND | ND | ND |
| | | V(K) – market value of capital | | | |
| | | V(E) – market value of equity | | | |
| | | K – total capital | | | |
| | | E – equity | | | |
| SVA | ΔV(E) = DIV - I | SVA – Shareholder Value Added | ND | ND | ND |
| | | ΔV(E) – increase of market value of equity | | | |
| | | DIV – dividends paid during the year | | | |
| | | I – net investments of stockholders | | | |

Source: Author's own analysis based on Wratislavia Bio Sp. z o.o.'s financial data, and A. Jaki. 2013. *Pomiar i ocena efektywności kreowania wartości w przedsiębiorstwie*. Finanse, Rynki Finansowe, Ubezpieczenia no. 59 (760). Szczecin: 135.

The last group of measures includes relative market measures of efficiency (Table 49). They can be calculated for companies listed on the stock exchange. Wratislavia-Bio Sp. z o.o. is not a joint-stock company, so this measure was not calculated in this case.

**Table 49. Relative market measures of efficiency in Wratislavia-Bio in 2008-2010**

| MARKET MEASURES OF EFFICIENCY | | |
|---|---|---|
| Relative measures | | |
| TSR | $[(P_1 - P_0) + DPS]/P_0$ | TSR – total shareholder return (return on shares) |
| | | $P_1 P_0$ – market price of shares as of the beginning and end of the period |
| | | DPS – dividend per share paid in a given period |

Source: Author's own analysis based on Wratislavia Bio Sp. z o.o.'s financial data, and A. Jaki. 2013. *Pomiar i ocena efektywności kreowania wartości w przedsiębiorstwie*. Finanse, Rynki Finansowe, Ubezpieczenia no. 59 (760). Szczecin: 135.

## 3.3. Executing the Restructuring Process

Due to the company's situation and the increasing crisis, it was necessary to introduce drastic measures aiming at the improvement of the very difficult situation. The company ceased operating; it had an advanced production line which had been constructed several years before, financed with resources from an investment credit. As the company stopped operating, it was also necessary to perform debt restructuring. Apart from covering its fixed costs, the company also had to pay its liabilities to the bank. The main property of the company was the production line and its infrastructure, for example of containers used to store manufactured products. At the end of 2010, the company had no signed contracts or even short-term agreements that could at least slightly change its situation. It was necessary to take strong measures to perform company restructuring.

A restructuring process requires an action plan with a schedule and the list of persons responsible for the execution of specific actions. The plan of restructuring should include the following information:

1. The analysis of the company's difficult situation,
2. Planned restructuring actions along with their cost,
3. The schedule of implementation in business practice.

All actions related to restructuring should be regularly checked in order to maintain short periods between each action controlling plan assumptions with its execution. Such a plan was prepared and implemented in Wratislavia-Bio Sp. z. o.o.

The company restructuring started in 2011. The period of 2008–2010 was critical for the decision about restructuring. The situation of Wratislavia-Bio Sp. z. o.o. was very difficult. The company generated a net loss, the level of revenues from sales dramatically decreased, there were no signed agreements, contracts for the delivery of ready products, and, as a result, the company had to settle its liabilities with delay or could not do it at all due to the lack of finances. Apart from preparing the plan of restructuring, to make further operations possible, it was also necessary to aim at signing contracts for deliveries and find financing for current liabilities.

In 2011, as a part of the restructuring process, the company management board was changed, and the company hired managers who knew the industry and its business reality. New employment in the company which was in a very difficult situation was not easy, but it was a success, and improved the limited (due to history of the period of 2008–2010) opportunity for the change in the situation of the company.

In 2012, the management board made a decision to reorganize the company operations and increase efficiency of production line functioning. Based on the management team's experience, initially, the company tried to sign contracts for one-time deliveries to customers, as, with the history of the company, it was impossible to sign different contracts at that time. Finding one-time orders was a success and was intended to present the company as a reliable partner and allow for future deliveries and, possibly, signing agreements for longer periods. The next step related to one-time deliveries was to ensure capital for the purchase of raw materials necessary in the production process.

**Table 50. Profit and loss account by function in Wratislavia-Bio Sp. z. o.o. in the first and second quarter of 2012**

| **Profit and loss account** | **1st quarter of 2012** | **2nd quarter of 2012** |
|---|---|---|
| Net revenues from sales | 44 151 261.52 | 124 216 704.52 |
| Cost of products, goods, and materials sold | 41 692 179.97 | 110 552 789.28 |
| **Profit (loss) on sales** | **2 459 081.55** | **13 663 915.24** |
| Cost of sales | 451 669.59 | 482 103.36 |
| Overhead costs | 1 443 690.21 | 1 149 251.40 |
| **Profit (loss) on sales** | **563 721.75** | **12 032 560.48** |
| Other operating revenues | 0.00 | 0.00 |
| Other operating expenses | 44 513.83 | 80 019.98 |
| Operating profit (loss) | 519 207.92 | 11 952 540.50 |
| Financial revenues | 145 438.75 | 13 540.86 |
| Financial expenses | 2 029 804.61 | 3 539 174.59 |
| **Profit (loss) on economic activities** | **-1 365 157.94** | **8 426 906.77** |
| Result on extraordinary events | | |
| **Gross profit (loss)** | **-1 365 157.94** | **8 426 906.77** |
| Income tax | | |
| **Net profit (loss)** | **-1 365 157.94** | **8 426 906.77** |

Source: Wratislavia-Bio Sp. z o.o.'s financial data.

As a result, at the turn of 2011, the company obtained resources from an investment fund, what was supposed to allow to recommission the installation production and to buy materials for production which are necessary for a one-time delivery. This capital was a crucial point of restructuring, and it was possible to obtain it thanks to the company assets which could serve as a security for provided financing. The deliveries were successful, which significantly affected the way the company was perceived on the market. Executed deliveries led to new development opportunities in the form of new deliveries. As a result, sales increased dynamically – just as the need for capital. In 2012, the company signed its first year-long contracts for the delivery of ready products, which, together with the improved financial situation, allowed the company to obtain debt financing in the form of two advances. Also, it was easier to receive a bank credit. The process of restructuring is often related to a proper cooperation with banks, aiming at restructuring of owned credits or obtaining new financing – a so-called relationship banking[171]. This ensured resources for manufacturing and executing customer contracts. In the first quarter, the company obtained resourced for executed deliveries, but it was only in the second quarter (Table 50) when the company sales significantly increased due to the obtained capital and signed contracts for product deliveries. In the first quarter, net revenues from sales increased. A positive operating result occurred, but the company continued to generate a net loss. The situation changed in the second quarter of 2012.

The joint capital obtained in 2012 amounted to PLN 151,000,000 and ensured the possibility to resume production and execute the restructuring plan in accordance with the schedule.

**Table 51. Profit and loss account by function in Wratislavia-Bio Sp. z. o.o. in the third and fourth quarter of 2012**

| **Profit and loss account** | **3rd quarter of 2012** | **4th quarter of 2012** |
|---|---|---|
| Net revenues from sales | 152 937 388.67 | 156 858 629.97 |
| Cost of products, goods, and materials sold | 137 653 819.70 | 140 771 072.89 |
| **Profit (loss) on sales** | **15 283 568.97** | **16 087 557.08** |
| Cost of sales | 677 862.08 | 637 435.15 |
| Overhead costs | 1 971 881.78 | 3 352 690.88 |
| **Profit (loss) on sales** | **12 633 825.11** | **12 097 431.05** |
| Other operating revenues | 11 571.31 | 7 758 992.67 |
| Other operating expenses | 999 148.89 | 4 036 845.24 |
| Operating profit (loss) | 11 646 247.53 | 15 819 578.48 |
| Financial revenues | 13 364.78 | 43 720.17 |
| Financial expenses | 4 374 462.64 | 5 641 708.41 |
| **Profit (loss) on economic activities** | **7 285 149.67** | **10 221 590.24** |
| Result on extraordinary events | 0.00 | 0.00 |
| **Gross profit (loss)** | **7 285 149.67** | **10 221 590.24** |
| Income tax | 0.00 | -3 052 231.36 |
| **Net profit (loss)** | **7 285 149.67** | **13 273 821.60** |

Source: Wratislavia-Bio Sp. z o.o.'s financial data.

[171] H. Pernsteiner, and J. Węcławski, *Factors of Influence on Relationship Banking of Polish Firms*. In: K. Jajuga, L. Orlowski, K. Staehr (eds.) *Contemporary Trends and Challenges in Finance*. Springer 2017 *Proceedings in Business and Economics*: 203-211.

The next quarters of 2012 (Table 51) were a continuation of previously taken actions. The company regained its financial stability, had a financial liquidity, and could regulate its liabilities to the customers and financial institutions.

The achieved net profit was spent to settle liabilities to customers and financial institutions, as well as to finance company turnover. Sales increased in 2012 and got even better in 2013. As a result of achieved good financial results in 2012, the negotiation position of the company changed dramatically. That is why, the company signed contracts for 2013 for bigger deliveries than previously.

### 3.3.1. The Analysis of the Company Situation during Restructuring

The initial analysis and ratio analysis were conducted before the restructuring process. In order to perform a comparative analysis, necessary values were calculated during and after the actions included in the restructuring plan.

In 2011 (Table 52), fixed assets were significantly higher than current assets. In the following years, due to intensified operations of the company, the relations between fixed and current assets changed. In 2014, fixed assets were higher than current assets.

It is clearly visible that the change of equity was beneficial – it significantly increased in 2011–2014 as a result of restructuring and achieved net profits. Thus, the liabilities reached the highest value in 2012, and gradually decreased in the years that followed.

Having performed horizontal and vertical analyzes of the company (Table 53), it shall be emphasized that equity increased and the problem of liabilities was solved. Since 2012, the company situation has stabilized and become more predictable. The risk of bankruptcy or winding-up was significantly decreased. These are the positive results of restructuring.

**Table 52. Wratislavia Bio Sp. z o.o.'s balance sheet for 2011–2014 (thousands of PLN)**

| **ASSETS** | **2011** | **2012** | **2013** | **2014** |
|---|---|---|---|---|
| **A. FIXED ASSETS** | **74 122.00** | **85 919.00** | **91 347.42** | **84 296.10** |
| I INTANGIBLE ASSETS | 136.00 | 57.00 | 26.40 | 16.00 |
| II TANGIBLE FIXED ASSETS | 72 762.00 | 76 813.00 | 84 443.46 | 81 282.51 |
| III LONG-TERM RECEIVABLES | | | | |
| IV LONG-TERM INVESTMENTS | | 630.00 | 942.94 | 942.94 |
| V LONG-TERM PREPAYMENTS | 1 224.00 | 8 419.00 | 5 934.62 | 2 054.65 |
| **B. CURRENT ASSETS** | **8 812.00** | **93 304.00** | **50 956.21** | **59 557.46** |
| I INVENTORY | 4 349.00 | 14 111.00 | 13 974.10 | 11 261.00 |
| II SHORT-TERM RECEIVABLES | 3 236.00 | 67 081.00 | 30 762.56 | 34 473.50 |
| III SHORT-TERM INVESTMENTS | 1 208.00 | 11 406.00 | 5 720.65 | 13 371.66 |
| IV SHORT-TERM PREPAYMENTS | 19.00 | 706.00 | 498.90 | 451.30 |
| TOTAL ASSETS | 82 934.00 | 179 223.00 | 142 303.63 | 143 853.56 |
| **LIABILITIES** | **2011** | **2012** | **2013** | **2014** |
| **A. EQUITY** | **18 261.00** | **25 868.00** | **40 202.91** | **62 298.54** |
| **B. LIABILITIES AND PROVISIONS FOR LIABILITIES** | **64 673.00** | **153 355.00** | **102 100.72** | **81 555.02** |
| I PROVISIONS FOR LIABILITIES | 1 044.00 | 3 488.00 | 2 290.36 | 3 769.03 |
| II LONG-TERM LIABILITIES | | | 41 937.87 | |
| III SHORT-TERM LIABILITIES | 63 629.00 | 149 867.00 | 57 872.49 | 77 741.51 |
| IV ACCRUALS | | | | 44.48 |
| **TOTAL LIABILITIES** | **82 934.00** | **179 223.00** | **142 303.63** | **143 853.56** |

Source: Wratislavia-Bio Sp. z o.o.'s financial data.

Further analysis of financial documents, after analysing balance sheets, focused on the profit and loss account by function (Table 54).

In 2012–2013 (Table 54), there was an increase of revenues to their maximum level of PLN 484,500,000. The operating profit reported in 2011 was not repeated in the following years (Figure 24). In 2012-2014, the operating profit amounted to, respectively: PLN 39,940,000; PLN 30,590,000; and 36,380,000. In the period of 2012–2014, the company reported a significant net profit. As it had suffered a loss before, in the situation of achieving a profit, it could qualify loss from previous years as tax deductible.

## Table 53. Horizontal and vertical analysis of Wratislavia Bio Sp z o.o.'s balance sheet

| **Balance sheet item/year** | **2010** | **2011** | | | | **2012** | | | | **2013** | | | | **2014** | | | |
|---|---|---|---|---|---|---|---|---|---|---|---|---|---|---|---|---|---|
| **ASSETS** | Value (in thousands of PLN) | Value (in thousands of PLN) | Dynamics in 2012/2011 | Change rate 2012/2011 | Structure in 2011 | Value (in thousands of PLN) | Dynamics in 2012/2011 | Change rate 2012/2011 | Structure in 2012 | Value (in thousands of PLN) | Dynamics in 2013/2012 | Change rate 2013/2012 | Structure in 2013 | Value (in thousands of PLN) | Dynamics in 2014/2013 | Change rate 2014/2013 | Structure in 2014 |
| **A. FIXED ASSETS** | **77731.9** | **74 122.00** | **0.95** | **-0.05** | **0.89** | **85 919.00** | **1.16** | **0.16** | **0.48** | **91 347.42** | **1.06** | **0.06** | **0.64** | **84 296.10** | **0.92** | **-0.08** | **0.59** |
| I INTANGIBLE ASSETS | 252.5 | 136.00 | **0.54** | **-0.46** | 0,00 | 57.00 | 0.42 | **-0.58** | **0.00** | 26.40 | 0.46 | **-0.54** | 0.01 | 16.00 | 0.61 | **-0.39** | 0.01 |
| II TANGIBLE ASSETS | 77479.4 | 72 762.00 | **0.94** | **-0.06** | 0.98 | 76 813.00 | 1.06 | **0.06** | **0.89** | 84 443.46 | 1.10 | **0.10** | 0.92 | 81 282.51 | 0.96 | **-0.04** | 0.96 |
| III LONG-TERM RECEIVABLES | | | | | 0.00 | | | | | | | **-1.00** | | | | **-1.00** | |
| IV LONG-TERM INVESTMENTS | | | | | 0.00 | 630.00 | | | | 942.94 | | **-1.00** | | 942.94 | | **-1.00** | |
| V LONG-TERM PREPAYMENTS | | 1 224.00 | | | 0.02 | 8 419.00 | | | **0.10** | 5 934.62 | 0.70 | **-0.30** | | 2 054.65 | 0.35 | **-0.65** | |

| **Balance sheet item/year** | **2010** | **2011** | | | | **2012** | | | | **2013** | | | | **2014** | | | |
|---|---|---|---|---|---|---|---|---|---|---|---|---|---|---|---|---|---|
| **ASSETS** | Value (in thousands of PLN) | Value (in thousands of PLN) | Dynamics in 2012/2011 | Change rate 2012/2011 | Structure in 2011 | Value (in thousands of PLN) | Dynamics in 2012/2011 | Change rate 2012/2011 | Structure in 2012 | Value (in thousands of PLN) | Dynamics in 2013/2012 | Change rate 2013/2012 | Structure in 2013 | Value (in thousands of PLN) | Dynamics in 2014/2013 | Change rate 2014/2013 | Structure in 2014 |
| B. CURRENT ASSETS | **3531** | **8 812.00** | **2.50** | **1.50** | **0.11** | **93 304.00** | **10.59** | **9.59** | **0.52** | **50 956.21** | **0.55** | **-0.45** | **0.36** | **59 557.46** | **1.17** | **0.17** | **0.41** |
| I INVENTORY | 2262.5 | 4 349.00 | **1.92** | **0.92** | 0.49 | 14 111.00 | 3.24 | **2.24** | 0.15 | 13 974.10 | 0.99 | **-0.01** | 0.27 | 11 261.00 | 0.81 | **-0.19** | 0.19 |
| II SHORT-TERM RECEIVABLES | 737.4 | 3 236.00 | **4.39** | **3.39** | 0.37 | 67 081.00 | 20.73 | **19.73** | 0.72 | 30 762.56 | 0.46 | **-0.54** | 0.60 | 34 473.50 | 1.12 | **0.12** | 0.58 |
| III SHORT-TERM INVESTMENTS | 492.6 | 1 208.00 | **2.45** | **1.45** | 0.14 | 11 406.00 | 9.44 | **8.44** | 0.12 | 5 720.65 | 0.50 | **-0.50** | 0.11 | 13 371.66 | 2.34 | **1.34** | 0.22 |
| IV SHORT-TERM PREPAYMENTS | 38.5 | 19.00 | **0.49** | **-0.51** | 0.00 | 706.00 | 37.16 | **36.16** | 0.01 | 498.90 | 0.71 | **-0.29** | 0.01 | 451.30 | 0.90 | **-0.10** | 0.01 |
| **TOTAL ASSETS** | **81262.9** | **82 934.00** | **1.02** | **0.02** | **1.00** | **179 223.00** | **2.16** | **1.16** | **1.00** | **142 303.63** | **0.79** | **-0.21** | | **143 853.56** | **1.01** | **0.01** | |
| **LIABILITIES** | 2010 | **2011** | **1.00** | | | **2012** | | | | **2013** | | **-1.00** | | **2014** | | **-1.00** | |
| A. EQUITY | **25203** | **18 261.00** | **0.72** | **-0.28** | **0.22** | **25 868.00** | **1.42** | **0.42** | **0.14** | **40 202.91** | **1.55** | **0.55** | **0.28** | **62 298.54** | **1.55** | **0.55** | **0.43** |

## Table 53. (Continued)

| Balance sheet item/year | 2010 | 2011 | | | | 2012 | | | | 2013 | | | | 2014 | | | |
|---|---|---|---|---|---|---|---|---|---|---|---|---|---|---|---|---|---|
| **ASSETS** | Value (in thousands of PLN) | Value (in thousands of PLN) | Dynamics in 2012/2011 | Change rate 2012/2011 | Structure in 2011 | Value (in thousands of PLN) | Dynamics in 2012/2011 | Change rate 2012/2011 | Structure in 2012 | Value (in thousands of PLN) | Dynamics in 2013/2012 | Change rate 2013/2012 | Structure in 2013 | Value (in thousands of PLN) | Dynamics in 2014/2013 | Change rate 2014/2013 | Structure in 2014 |
| B. LIABILITIES AND PROVISIONS FOR LIABILITIES | **56059.9** | **64 673.00** | **1.15** | **0.15** | **0.78** | **153 355.00** | **2.37** | **1.37** | **0.86** | **102 100.72** | **0.67** | **-0.33** | **0.72** | **81 555.02** | **0.80** | **-0.20** | **0.57** |
| I PROVISIONS FOR LIABILITIES | 1364.3 | 1 044.00 | **0.77** | **-0.23** | 0.02 | 3 488.00 | 3.34 | **2.34** | 0.02 | 2 290.36 | 0.66 | **-0.34** | 0.02 | 3 769.03 | 1.65 | **0.65** | 0.05 |
| II LONG-TERM LIABILITIES | 34125.5 | | **0.00** | **-1.00** | 0.00 | | | **-1.00** | 0.00 | 41 937.87 | #DZIEL/0! | **#DZIEL/0!** | 0.41 | | 0.00 | **-1.00** | 0.00 |
| III SHORT-TERM LIABILITIES | 20570.1 | 63 629.00 | **3.09** | **2.09** | 0.98 | 149 867.00 | 2.36 | **1.36** | | 57 872.49 | 0.39 | **-0.61** | 0.57 | 77 741.51 | 1.34 | **0.34** | 0.95 |
| IV ACCRUALS | | | | **-1.00** | 0.00 | | | **-1.00** | 0.00 | | | **-1.00** | | 44.48 | | **-1.00** | |
| **TOTAL LIABILITES** | **81262.9** | **82 934.00** | **1.02** | **0.02** | **1.00** | **179 223.00** | **2.16** | **1.16** | **1.00** | **142 303.63** | **0.79** | **-0.21** | **1.00** | **143 853.56** | **1.01** | **0.01** | **1.00** |

Source: Wratislavia-Bio Sp. z o.o.'s financial data.

**Table 54. Profit and loss account by function in Wratislavia Bio Sp. z. o.o. in 2008–2010 (thousands of PLN)**

| **Profit and loss account** | **2011** | **2012** | **2013** | **2014** |
|---|---|---|---|---|
| Net revenues from sales | 29 989.00 | 478 164.00 | 484 526.43 | 380 291.97 |
| Costs of products, goods, and materials sold | 29 037.00 | 430 670.00 | 437 627.36 | 330 046.41 |
| **Profit (loss) on sales** | **952.00** | **47 494.00** | **46 899.07** | **50 245.56** |
| Cost of sales | 697.00 | 2 249.00 | 4 005.93 | 4 349.46 |
| Overhead costs | 4 259.00 | 7 918.00 | 8 615.03 | 9 258.84 |
| Profit (loss) on sales | -4 004.00 | 37 327.00 | 34 278.11 | 36 637.26 |
| Other operating revenues | 1 279.00 | 7 771.00 | 3 403.69 | 1 700.64 |
| Other operating expenses | 18 669.00 | 5 160.00 | 7 087.10 | 1 954.51 |
| **Operating profit (loss)** | **-21 394.00** | **39 938.00** | **30 594.70** | **36 383.39** |
| Financial revenues | 2 921.00 | 216.00 | 496.65 | 861.40 |
| Financial expenses | 8 497.00 | 15 585.00 | 11 250.10 | 9 394.63 |
| **Profit (loss) on economic activities** | **-26 970.00** | **24 569.00** | **19 841.25** | **27 850.16** |
| Result on extraordinary events | | | | |
| **Gross profit (loss)** | **-26 970.00** | **24 569.00** | **19 841.25** | **27 850.16** |
| OTHER STATUTORY REDUCTIONS IN PROFIT (INCREASES OF LOSS) | 3 663.00 | -3 052.00 | 5 505.68 | 5 754.53 |
| **Net profit (loss)** | **-23 307.00** | **27 621.00** | **14 335.57** | **22 095.63** |

Source: Wratislavia-Bio Sp. z o.o.'s financial data.

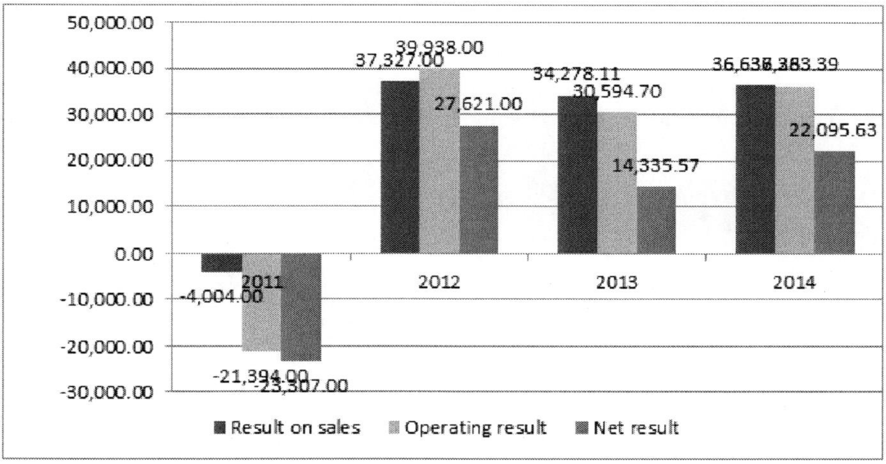


Source: Wratislavia-Bio Sp. z o.o.'s financial data.

Figure 24. Profit and loss account in Wratislavia Bio Sp. z. o.o. in 2011–2014 (thousands of PLN).

**Table 55. Cash flow account in Wratislavia Bio Sp. z o.o in 2010 (thousands of PLN)**

| No | Change: | 2011 | 2012 | 2013 | 2014 |
|---|---|---|---|---|---|
| 1 | Net cash flows from operating activities | 1 851.00 | 32 743.00 | 13 502.68 | 24 309.96 |
| 2 | Net cash flows from investment in the amount of | -1.00 | -27 567.00 | -6 479.01 | -19.73 |
| 3 | Net cash flows from financial activities in the amount of | -1 134.00 | -5 929.00 | -6 698.24 | -16 956.37 |
| 4 | Total net cash flows (1+/-2+/-3) | 716.00 | -753.00 | 325.43 | 7 333.86 |

Source: Wratislavia Bio Sp. z o.o.'s financial data.

**Table 56. The analysis of cash flows in the company, with surpluses and deficiencies from all activities (operating, investment, and financial ones) taken into consideration**

| | Cases | | | | | | | |
|---|---|---|---|---|---|---|---|---|
| **Stream type** | 1 | 2 | 3 | 4 | 5 | 6 | 7 | 8 |
| **Phase type** | A mature phase | | | | A transitory phase | | A phase of threat | |
| **Operating** | + | + | + | + | - | - | - | - |
| **Investment** | + | - | + | - | + | - | + | - |
| **Financial** | + | - | - | + | + | + | - | - |

Source: D. Wędzki. 2010. Wykorzystanie rachunku przepływów pieniężnych do analizy finansowej, „Rachunkowość" 2010, no. 1, E. Mioduchowska-Jaroszewicz. 2012. Ocena przepływów pieniężnych w grupach kapitałowych, Zeszyty Naukowe Uniwersytetu Szczecińskiego. *Finanse. Rynki finansowe. Ubezpieczenia* 56: 155-171.

The next element included an analysis of a cash flow account in 2010 (Table 55).

In 2012-2014, the company situation significantly improved. The company started to function and manufacture products with the use of a significant part of its production force. As a result, an improvement in the cash flow account was reported (Table 56). There was a significant increase of net cash flows from operating activities (to the level of PLN 32,740,000 in 2012 and PLN 24,310,000 in 2014). Net cash flows from investment and financial activities were negative. The total value of net cash flows was the highest in 2014 and amounted to PLN 7,330,000.

Considering the company situation and the analysis including the cases of balances of individual parts of the cash flow account (Table 57), it is justified to categorize Wratislavia-Bio Sp. z. o.o. as the second case. It means that the company has a high profitability and uses its profits for development and settlement of liabilities.

The initial analysis was followed by a ratio analysis, allowing to evaluate the company situation in the restructuring process and check if it has improved.

### 3.3.2. Liquidity Analysis

The liquidity analysis calculated ratios for the period of 2011–2014 (Table 57). The situation visibly improved each year. In 2011, the current ratio was on a critically low level and amounted to merely 0.14. In 2012, after restructuring, the current ratio increased to 0.62, and achieved the highest value in 2013. Later, the ratio slightly decreased to the level of 0.77. The quick ratio changed in the similar way as the current ratio. However, the cash to debt ratio regularly increased each year and amounted to 0.17 in 2014.

To a large extent, the problems of the company related with liquidity (Figure 25) were solved in the first year of restructuring (2012). The company gained and increased resources necessary to carry out its obligations. The analysis of the company liquidity situation was followed by a debt analysis.

**Table 57. Liquidity ratios in Wratislavia-Bio in 2011-2014**

| Ratio name | Calculation method | 2011 | 2012 | 2013 | 2014 |
|---|---|---|---|---|---|
| Current ratio | Current assets/Shor-term liabilities | 0.14 | 0.62 | 0.88 | 0.77 |
| Quick ratio | (Current assets – Inventory – Short-term prepayments)/ Short-term liabilities | 0.07 | 0.52 | 0.63 | 0.62 |
| Cash to debt ratio | Short-term investments/Short-term liabilities | 0.02 | 0.08 | 0.10 | 0.17 |

Source: Wratislavia Bio Sp. z o.o.'s financial data.

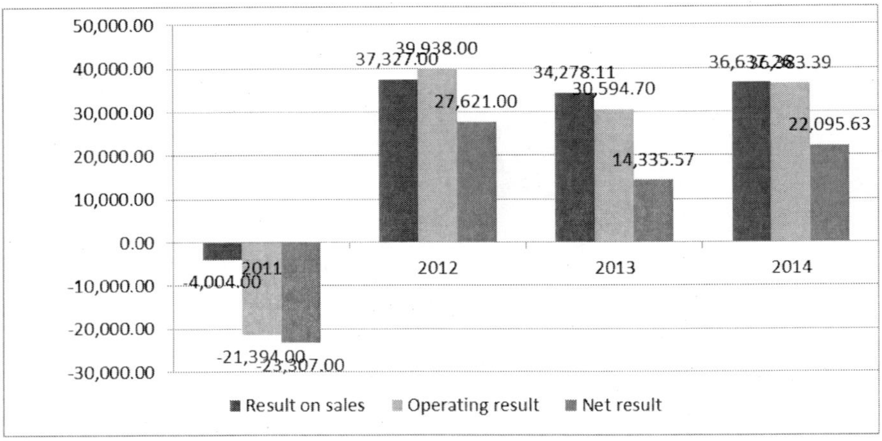


Source: Wratislavia Bio Sp. z o.o.'s financial data.

Figure 25. Shaping of liquidity ratios in Wratislavia-Bio in 2011-2014.

### 3.3.3. Debt Analysis

The company debt was the highest in 2011 and 2012. Then, it significantly decreased (Table 58). The debt ratio reached the level of 0.54 in 2014. This indicates the improvement of the financial situation of the company and the decrease of debt as compared to the earlier years (2011–2013), when the values were high enough and amounted to, respectively: 0.77, 0.84, 0.70.

After the debt analysis, the efficiency of activity was analysed.

**Table 58. Debt ratios in Wratislavia-Bio in 2011-2014**

| Ratio name | Calculation method | 2011 | 2012 | 2013 | 2014 |
|---|---|---|---|---|---|
| Debt ratio | Total liabilities/Total assets | 0.77 | 0.84 | 0.70 | 0.54 |
| Debt to liquidity ratio | Total liabilities/equity | 3.48 | 5.79 | 2.48 | 1.25 |
| Long term debt to equity | Long-term liabilities/equity | 0.00 | 0.00 | 1.04 | 0.00 |
| Fixed assets debt | Tangible current assets/Long-term liabilities | | | 2.01 | |

Source: Wratislavia Bio Sp. z o.o.'s financial data.

The debt ratio decreased and reached the level of 1.25 in 2014. Before that, its values had been significantly higher (3.48 in 2011). Due to the lack of long-term liabilities in some of the years, the long-term debt ratio and fixed assets debt ratio were calculated only in 2013.

### 3.3.4. Activity Efficiency (Turnover) Analysis

The analysis included a turnover of receivables, inventory, and liabilities (Table 59). The values of days sales outstanding were the highest in 2012. Then, they decreased and reached the level of 32.63 days. That means that the company improved the collection of receivables and limited the payment deadlines.

**Table 59. Activity efficiency ratios in Wratislavia-Bio Sp. z. o.o. in 2011-2014**

| Ratio name | Calculation method | 2011 | 2012 | 2013 | 2014 |
|---|---|---|---|---|---|
| Asset turnover ratio | Net revenues from sale/Total assets | 0.36 | 2.67 | 3.40 | 2.64 |
| Receivables turnover ratio | Net revenues from sale/Total receivables | 9.27 | 7.13 | 15.75 | 11.03 |
| Days sales outstanding | Total receivables*360/ Net revenues from sale | 38.85 | 50.50 | 22.86 | 32.63 |
| Inventory turnover ratio | Net revenues from sale/Inventory | 6.90 | 33.89 | 34.67 | 33.77 |
| Days inventory turnover ratio | Inventory*360/Net revenues from sale | 52.21 | 10.62 | 10.38 | 10.66 |
| Ratio of paying back liabilities in days | Short-term liabilities*360/Net revenues from sale | 763.83 | 112.83 | 43.00 | 73.59 |
| Cash ratio | Days receivables turnover ratio + days cycle of inventory – days liabilities turnover ratio | -672.77 | -51.70 | -9.76 | -30.30 |

Source: Wratislavia Bio Sp. z o.o.'s financial data.

**Table 60. Activity efficiency ratios in Wratislavia-Bio Sp. z. o.o. in 2011-2014**

| **Activity efficiency (turnover) ratios** | | | | |
|---|---|---|---|---|
| Ratio/year | 2011 | 2012 | 2013 | 2014 |
| Receivables turnover | 38.85 | 50.50 | 22.86 | 32.63 |
| Inventory turnover | 52.21 | 10.62 | 10.38 | 10.66 |
| Inventory turnover | 763.83 | 112.83 | 43.00 | 73.59 |

Source: Wratislavia Bio Sp. z o.o.'s financial data.

After the commissioning of production, in 2012-2014, the inventory cycle was at a stable, low level of around 10 days.

The ratios related to the turnover of liabilities in days reached the highest level – 43 days – in 2012, and then they decreased to ca. 74 days. Earlier, in 2011 and 2012, due to company problems resulting from previous periods and current ones, the liability ratio was on an inaccessible level. The company did not operate; thus, it had no resources to pay its liabilities. The cash cycle definitely improved.

The above data can lead to the conclusion (Table 60) that, first, the company obtains resources from the sale of products (receivables), and then it pays its liabilities. Therefore, it does not need additional financing to settle its liabilities. The company has resources and before it repays its liabilities, the money can be used for a short period of time. In 2014, the liability turnover deadline was quite long. It could be shorter for a better cooperation with the customers.

The analysis of activity efficiency was followed by the analysis of company profitability.

### 3.3.5. Profitability Analysis

In 2011, the company reported negative values of profitability ratios (Table 62). It was caused by the difficult situation of the company and stopped operations in that year. The company generated losses and, as a result, ratios took negative values. After restructuring actions, the company resumed its operations and generated a net profit. In 2012, the ratio values significantly improved. Return on sales amounted to 6%, return on assets – to 15%, and return on equity – to 107%. The achieved net profit in one year (2012) was higher than equity from that year.

Net return on sales was the best in 2012 and 2014; return on assets – also in 2012 and 2014; return on equity – in 2012, and return on investment – in 2014 (Table 61).

Profitability ratios are a perfect reflection of the results of restructuring. The financial situation of the company improved in a given period. As a result, it was possible to achieve positive net financial results, which can be reflected in profitability ratios for 2012–2014 (Figure 26).

**Table 61. Profitability ratios in Wratislavia-Bio Sp. z. o.o. in 2011-2014**

| Ratio name | Calculation method | 2011 | 2012 | 2013 | 2014 |
|---|---|---|---|---|---|
| Net return on sales | Net income/Net revenues from sale | -0.78 | 0.06 | 0.03 | 0.06 |
| Return on assets | Net income/Total assets | -0.28 | 0.15 | 0.10 | 0.15 |
| Return on equity | Net income/Total assets | -1.28 | 1.07 | 0.36 | 0.35 |
| Return on investment | Operating result/Total assets | -0.26 | 0.22 | 0.21 | 0.25 |

Source: Wratislavia Bio Sp. z o.o.'s financial data.

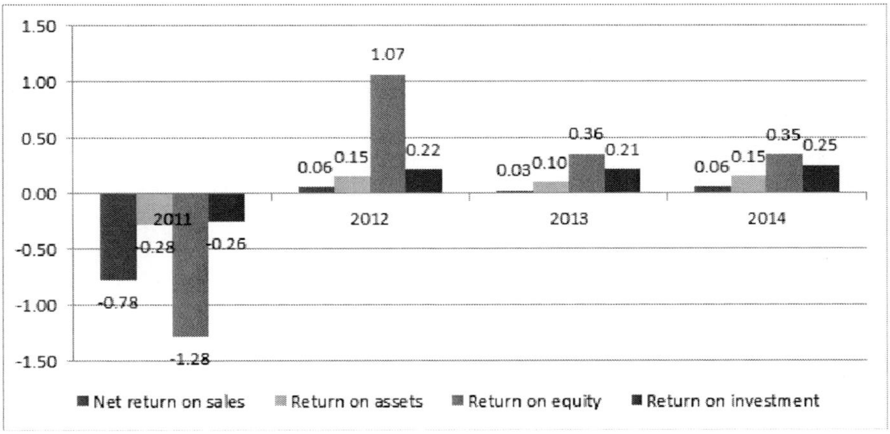


Source: Wratislavia Bio Sp. z o.o.'s financial data.

Figure 26. Shaping of profitability ratios in Wratislavia-Bio Sp. z. o.o. in 2011-2014.

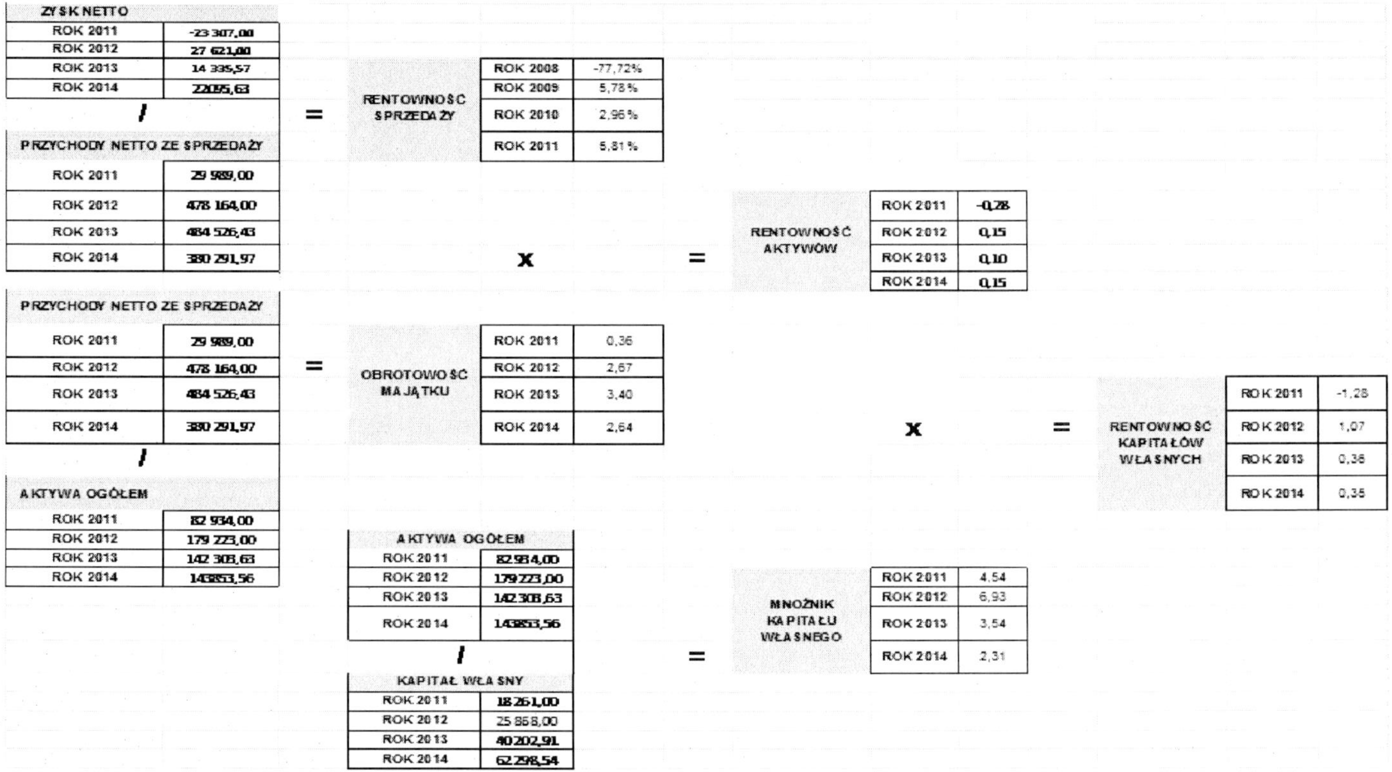


Source: Author's own analysis based on Wratislavia Bio Sp. z o.o.'s financial data.

Figure 27. DuPont model in 2008–2010 in Wratislavia-Bio Sp. z. o. o.

The analysis of profitability ratios is complemented with the DuPont model, which reflects what can be changed in a company for the optimization of equity profitability (Figure 27). For the improvement of ROE, it is necessary to affect the multiplier of equity by increasing the company assets. It is also possible to influence the asset turnover by aiming at increasing the revenues from sale.

After the ratio analysis, the evaluation of restructuring was extended with additional ratios, including: net working capital, and a golden and silver rule of balance sheet.

A negative net working capital is an alarming value. When combined with a high ratio of days liabilities turnover in 2014 (Table 62), it means that the company has more liabilities than owned money. The financial results are very good, but there are also certain objections regarding the value of liabilities and the deadline for their repayment. The golden rule of balance sheet amounted even to 25% and 30% in 2011–2012, but it later increased to 74%. It means that the company mostly uses its equity and its situation is more stable and safe. The silver rule of balance sheet reached the value of 90% in 2013, but later, in the following year, it decreased with the level of the golden rule of balance sheet, reaching the level of 74%.

**Table 62. Shaping of net working capital and balance sheet rules in Wratislavia-Bio Sp. z o.o. in 2011-2014**

| **Ratio name** | **Calculation method** | **2011** | **2012** | **2013** | **2014** |
|---|---|---|---|---|---|
| Net working capital (in thousands of PLN) | KS-AT | -55 861.00 | -60 051.00 | -9 206.64 | -21 997.56 |
| Golden rule of balance sheet | (KW/AT)x100% | 0.25 | 0.30 | 0.44 | 0.74 |
| Silver rule of balance sheet | (KS/AT)x100% | 0.25 | 0.30 | 0.90 | 0.74 |

Source: Author's own analysis based on Wratislavia Bio Sp. z o.o.'s financial data.

The last element calculated for 2011–2014 in order to evaluate the situation of the company was the Altman's model adjusted to companies functioning on developing markets (Table 63). The result in 2011 was critical, it improved in 2012, but it was only in 2013 and 2014 that it reached a value above 5. The value of 5.5 is a border point, but the company did not reach this result in any of the analyzed years. It was close to this point in 2014, but its value was slightly lower and amounted to 5.29, which means that the restructuring process was a success, but that there was still a great risk of bankruptcy. In spite of a huge risk, the company functioned while strengthening its market position and increasing revenues in the following years.

**Table 63. Altman's model (for the companies on developing markets) in Wratislavia-Bio Sp. z. o.o.**

| **Ratio** | **Calculation method** | **2011** | **2012** | **2013** | **2014** |
|---|---|---|---|---|---|
| Altman's model for developing markets | EM score = 6.56 X1 + 3.26 X2 + 6.72 X3 + 1.05 X4 + 3.35 | -3.52 | 3.23 | 5.02 | 5.29 |
| X1 | KON/Total assets | -0.67 | -0.34 | -0.06 | -0.15 |
| X2 | Accumulated retained earnings/Total assets | -0.28 | 0.15 | 0.10 | 0.15 |
| X3 | EBIT/Total assets | -0.26 | 0.22 | 0.21 | 0.25 |
| X4 | Equity market value/debt book value | 0.29 | 0.17 | 0.40 | 0.80 |

Source: Author's own analysis based on Wratislavia-Bio Sp. z o.o.'s financial data

The results of EM score are interpreted in the following way:

- (0 – 5.5 > high risk of bankruptcy;
- (5.5 – ∞) low risk of bankruptcy.

The next calculations will include absolute and relative measures of efficiency in 2011–2014. In 2011, the absolute measures of efficiency (Table 64) were negative. In the following years, they significantly improved. All measures were positive in 2014, which stressed that the introduced restructuring procedures were successful. That year, EBIT amounted to PLN 36,380,000, EBITDA – to PLN 39,500,000, NOPAT – to PLN 29,470,000, and EBITDAAT – to PLN 32,040,000.

## Table 64. Absolute accounting measures of efficiency in Wratislavia-Bio in 2011-2014

| ACCOUNTING MEASURES OF EFFICIENCY | | | | | | |
|---|---|---|---|---|---|---|
| Absolute measures (in thousands of PLN) | | | | | | |
| EBIT | NP + INT + T | EBIT – Earnings Before Interest (Operating Profit) | 2011 | 2012 | 2013 | 2014 |
| | | NP – Net Profit | -21 394.00 | 39 938.00 | 30 594.70 | 36 383.39 |
| | | INT – Interest | | | | |
| | | T – Tax | | | | |
| EBITDA | EBIT + DEP | EBITDA – Earnings Before Interest, Taxes, Depreciation, and Amortization | -16 560.00 | 44 446.00 | 35 190.70 | 39 556.39 |
| | | EBIT – Earnings Before Interest (Operating Profit) | | | | |
| | | DEP – Depreciation | | | | |
| NOPAT | EBIT x (1 - T) | NOPAT – Net Operating Profit After Tax | -17 329.14 | 32 349.78 | 24 781.71 | 29 470.55 |
| | | EBIT – Earnings Before Interest (Operating Profit) | | | | |
| | | T – Tax | | | | |
| EBIDAAT | (EBIT + DEP) x (1 - T) | EBIDAAT – Earnings Before Interest, Depreciation and Amortization, After Taxes | -13 413.60 | 36 001.26 | 28 504.47 | 32 040.68 |
| | | EBIT – Earnings Before Interest (Operating Profit) | | | | |
| | | DEP – Depreciation | | | | |
| | | T – Tax | | | | |
| EPS | NP/number of shares | EPS – Earnings per Share | - | - | - | - |

Sources: Author's own analysis based on Wratislavia-Bio Sp. z o.o.'s financial data and A. Jaki. 2013. Pomiar i ocena efektywności kreowania wartości w przedsiębiorstwie. *Finanse, Rynki Finansowe, Ubezpieczenia* no. 59 (760). Szczecin: 135.

**Table 65. Relative accounting measures of efficiency in Wratislavia-Bio in 2011-2014**

| ACCOUNTING MEASURES OF EFFICIENCY | | | | | | |
|---|---|---|---|---|---|---|
| Relative measures | | | | | | |
| ROI | NOPAT/K | ROI – Return on Invested Capital | 2011 | 2012 | 2013 | 2014 |
| | | NOPAT – Net Operating Profit After Tax | -0.21 | 0.18 | 0.17 | 0.20 |
| | | K – Total capital (with the sum of liabilities included) | | | | |
| ROA | NP/A | ROA – net Return on Assets | -0.28 | 0.15 | 0.10 | 0.15 |
| | | NP – Net Profit | | | | |
| | | A – total assets | | | | |
| ROS | NP/S | ROS – Return on Sales | -0.78 | 0.06 | 0.03 | 0.06 |
| | | NP – Net Profit | | | | |
| | | S – net sales | | | | |
| ROE | NP/E | NP – Net Profit | -1.28 | 1.07 | 0.36 | 0.35 |
| | | E – Equity | | | | |
| DFL | (ROE - ROI)/ROI | DFL – Degree of Financial Leverage | 5.11 | 4.92 | 1.05 | 0.73 |
| | | ROE – Return on Equity | | | | |
| | | ROI – Return on Invested Capital | | | | |
| DOL | (S - VC)/EBIT | DOL – Degree of Operational Leverage | -0.04 | 1.19 | 1.53 | 1.38 |
| | | S – net sales | | | | |
| | | VC – Variable Costs | | | | |

Source: Author's own analysis based on Wratislavia Bio Sp. z o.o.'s financial data, and A. Jaki. 2013. Pomiar i ocena efektywności kreowania wartości w przedsiębiorstwie. *Finanse, Rynki Finansowe, Ubezpieczenia* no. 59 (760). Szczecin: 135.

## Table 66. Absolute financial measures of efficiency in Wratislavia-Bio in 2011-2014

| | | | | | | |
|---|---|---|---|---|---|---|
| **FINANCIAL MEASURES OF EFFICIENCY** | | | | | | |
| Absolute measures (in thousands of PLN) | | | | | | |
| FCF | NOPAT + DEP – I - ΔWC | FCF – Free Cash Flow | 2011 | 2012 | 2013 | 2014 |
| | | NOPAT – Net Operating Profit After Tax | 20 128.46 | 36 539.78 | -26 062.65 | 42 261.47 |
| | | DEP – Depreciation | | | | |
| | | I – investment capital | | | | |
| | | ΔWC – net change in working capital | | | | |
| FCFE | NP + DEP - I – ΔWC + ΔD | FCFE – Free Cash Flow to Equity | 11 195.06 | -49 698.22 | 23 993.99 | 64 330.32 |
| | | NP – Net Profit | | | | |
| | | DEP – Depreciation | | | | |
| | | I – investment capital | | | | |
| | | ΔWC – net change in working capital | | | | |
| | | ΔD – net increase in debt | | | | |
| GCF | NOPAT + DEP | GCF – Gross Cash Flow | -12 495.14 | 36 857.78 | 29 377.71 | 32 643.55 |
| | | NOPAT – Net Operating Profit After Tax | | | | |
| | | DEP – Depreciation | | | | |
| DCF | CF x $1/(1 + r)^n$ | DCF – Discounted Cash Flow | - | - | - | - |
| | | CF – Cash Flow | | | | |
| | | r – discount rate | | | | |
| | | n – number of years | | | | |

### Table 66. (Continued)

| | | | | | | |
|---|---|---|---|---|---|---|
| **FINANCIAL MEASURES OF EFFICIENCY** | | | | | | |
| Absolute measures (in thousands of PLN) | | | | | | |
| NPV | $\sum NCF \times 1/(1+r)^n - \sum I\ 1/(1+r)^n$ | NPV – Net Present Value | ND | ND | ND | ND |
| | | NCF – Net Cash Flow | | | | |
| | | r – discount rate | | | | |
| | | n – number of years | | | | |
| | | I – investment capital | | | | |
| CVA | K x (CFROI - WACC) = GCF - K x WACC | CVA – Cash Value Added | ND | 0.00 | 0.00 | 0.00 |
| | | K – total capital | | | | |
| | | CFROI – Cash Flow Return on Investment | | | | |
| | | WACC – Weighted Average Cost of Capital | | | | |
| | | GCF – Gross Cash Flow | | | | |

Source: Author's own analysis based on Wratislavia Bio Sp. z o.o.'s financial data, and A. Jaki. 2013. Pomiar i ocena efektywności kreowania wartości w przedsiębiorstwie. *Finanse, Rynki Finansowe, Ubezpieczenia* no. 59 (760). Szczecin: 135.

## Table 67. Relative financial measures of efficiency in Wratislavia-Bio in 2011-2014

| **FINANCIAL MEASURES OF EFFICIENCY** | | | | | | |
|---|---|---|---|---|---|---|
| Relative measures | | | | | | |
| IRR | $\sum NCF \times 1/(1 + IRR)^n = \sum I \times 1/(1 + IRR)^n$ | IRR – Internal Return Rate | 2011 | 2012 | 2013 | 2014 |
| | | NCF – Net Cash Flow | ND | ND | ND | ND |
| | | n – number of years | | | | |
| CFROI | $\sum NCF \times 1/(1 + CFROI)^n = \sum I \times 1/(1 + CFROI)^n$ | CFROI – Cash Flow Return on Investment | ND | ND | ND | ND |
| | | NCF – Net Cash Flow | | | | |
| | | n – number of years | | | | |
| WACC | $k_e \times E/K + k_d \times D/K$ | WACC – Weighted Average Cost of Capital | 13.35% | 10.40% | 11.27% | 12.08% |
| | | ke – cost of equity | | | | |
| | | kd – cost of foreign capital (debt) | | | | |
| | | E – equity | | | | |
| | | D – foreign capital (debt) | | | | |
| | | K – total capital | | | | |

Source: Author's own analysis based on Wratislavia Bio Sp. z o.o.'s financial data, and A. Jaki. 2013. Pomiar i ocena efektywności kreowania wartości w przedsiębiorstwie. *Finanse, Rynki Finansowe, Ubezpieczenia* no. 59 (760). Szczecin: 135.

## Table 68. Absolute market measures of efficiency in Wratislavia-Bio in 2011-2014

| | | | | | | |
|---|---|---|---|---|---|---|
| **MARKET MEASURES OF EFFICIENCY** | | | | | | |
| Absolute measures (in thousands of PLN) | | | | | | |
| $EVA^{TM}$ | K x (ROI - WACC) = NOPAT - K x WACC | $EVA^{TM}$ – Economic Value Added | 2011 | 2012 | 2013 | 2014 |
| | | K – total capital | -28 404.12 | 13 711.98 | 8 741.99 | 12 086.64 |
| | | ROI – Return on Investment | | | | |
| | | WACC – Weighted Average Cost of Capital | | | | |
| | | NOPAT – Net Operating Profit After Tax | | | | |
| EVC | E x (ROE - $k_e$) = NP - E x $k_e$ | EVC – Estimated Value Added | ND | ND | ND | ND |
| | | ROE – Return on Equity | | | | |
| | | ke – cost of equity | | | | |
| | | E – Equity | | | | |
| | | NP – Net Profit | | | | |
| MVA | V(K) - K = V(E) - E | MVA – Market Value Added | ND | ND | ND | ND |
| | | V(K) – market value of capital | | | | |
| | | V(E) – market value of equity | | | | |
| | | K – total capital | | | | |
| | | E – Equity | | | | |
| SVA | ΔV(E) = DIV - I | SVA – Shareholder Value Added | ND | ND | ND | ND |
| | | ΔV(E) – increase of market value of equity | | | | |
| | | DIV – dividends paid during the year | | | | |
| | | I – net investments of stockholders | | | | |

Source: Author's own analysis based on Wratislavia Bio Sp. z o.o.'s financial data, and A. Jaki. 2013. Pomiar i ocena efektywności kreowania wartości w przedsiębiorstwie. *Finanse, Rynki Finansowe, Ubezpieczenia* no. 59 (760). Szczecin: 135.

Next, the relative accounting measures of efficiency were calculated (Table 65). In 2011, the majority of ratios had negative values. A financial leverage was at a very high level due to significant financial liabilities. The period of 2012–2014 marks a significant improvement in the company situation, with high profitability of equity and assets, and acceptable net profitability. What is more, a decreased value of the financial leverage resulted from reduced financial liabilities. However, in spite of a better DFL value, the time of settling the liabilities is quite long, which results from liabilities turnover ratios. Throughout the three following years, the level of the financial leverage improved from a negative value and, in 2014, reached the level of 1.38.

Also, the absolute financial measures of efficiency were calculated (Table 66). The level of free cash flows was negative only in 2013. In 2014, it reached the highest value of PLN 42,260,000.

The Free Cash Flows for the owners were negative in 2012, but positive in the other periods. In 2014, they reached the highest value of PLN 64,330,000. The gross cash flows were negative in 2011. A record value was reached in 2012 and amounted to PLN 36,860,000.

Apart from financial measures of efficiency, also the relative measures of efficiency were calculated (Table 67). Among them, it was possible to indicate the values of a weighted average cost of capital (WACC). It was calculated as financial costs to total liabilities, so it included only the cost of debt.

The cost of debt was the highest in 2011 (13.35%), and the lowest in 2 2012 (10.40%). In 2012, this measure reached the value of 12.08%.

The next calculations included absolute market measures of efficiency (Table 68). For the company in this group of efficiency measures, it was possible to calculate only the economic value added (EVA$^{TM}$). In 2011, this value was negative. In the following years, its values were positive, and it reached the highest level in 2012 (PLN 13,710,000).

The last group of measures includes relative market measures of efficiency (Table 69). They can be calculated for companies listed on the stock exchange. Wratislavia-Bio Sp. z o.o. is not a joint-stock company, so this measure was not calculated in this case.

**Table 69. Relative market measures of efficiency in Wratislavia-Bio in 2011-2014**

| MARKET MEASURES OF EFFICIENCY | | |
|---|---|---|
| Relative measures | | |
| TSR | $[(P_1 - P_0) + DPS]/P_0$ | TSR – total shareholder return (return on shares) |
| | | $P_1P_0$ – market price of shares as of the beginning and end of the period |
| | | DPS – dividend per share paid in a given period |

Source: Author's own analysis based on Wratislavia Bio Sp. z o.o.'s financial data, and A. Jaki. 2013. Pomiar i ocena efektywności kreowania wartości w przedsiębiorstwie. *Finanse, Rynki Finansowe, Ubezpieczenia* no. 59 (760). Szczecin: 135.

## 3.4. Restructuring Tools and Effects

The main visible effect was that the company resumed production after a standby period. During the restructuring process, the company initially operated in a very difficult internal situation. One-time deliveries and achieved margins from sales allowed to quickly regain financial liquidity and trust on the market.

Considering the criteria of restructuring (Table 70), it should be explained that, from the perspective of the criterion of restructuring objectives, the company maintained its competitive advantage which resulted from owned technical infrastructure and the possibility to manufacture products meeting quality norms. Regarding the change rate, scope and area of restructuring, the applied process was a ground-breaking restructuring which changed many aspects of the conducted business activity, as well as it was a complex restructuring. It applied to company systems, such as the efficiency of production, supply, and the management system, as well as communication system used in the company. In order to perform restructuring actions, also the employment underwent a restructuring process. A new management board was hired and a qualified management team was employed.

**Table 70. Used types of restructuring in Wratislavia-Bio Sp. z. o.o. in 2010-2013**

| Restructuring criteria | | Performed |
|---|---|---|
| 1. | The criterion of restructuring objectives: | |
| | - Cost reduction, | |
| | - Maintaining a competitive advantage. | YES |
| 2. | A criterion of the scope and rate of changes: | |
| | - Groundbreaking restructuring, | YES |
| | - Incremental restructuring, | |
| | - Permanent restructuring, | |
| | - Restructuring conducted once in a given period. | |
| 3. | The criterion of reach | |
| | - Partial restructuring, | |
| | - Complex restructuring, | YES |
| | - Coordinated restructuring, | |
| | - Uncoordinated restructuring. | |
| 4. | The criterion of company systems | |
| | - Restructuring of a production system, | YES |
| | - Restructuring of a supply system, | YES |
| | - Restructuring of a management system, | YES |
| | - Restructuring of an information system. | YES |
| 5. | The criterion of production factors types: | |
| | - Restructuring of employment, | YES |
| | - Fixed assets restructuring, | |
| | - Subject of work restructuring. | |
| 6. | The criterion of strategic resources: | |
| | - Financial restructuring, | |
| | - Fixed assets restructuring, | |
| | - Restructuring of skills and labor resources. | |

Source: Author's own analysis based on Wratislavia-Bio Sp. z o.o.'s financial data.

The main tools selected to perform restructuring included TQM and Lean Management, as well as its other types (Table 71), based on introducing the habit of continuous improvement by streamlining processes, ensuring better communication, maintaining order in documentation and legal issues. Apart from that, the company also focused on rationalizing production and maintaining a necessary level of inventory.

**Table 71. Tools for company restructuring in Wratislavia-Bio Sp. z. o.o.**

| Used restructuring tools | Commentary |
|---|---|
| TQM | It was important to improve efficiency of operations in all organizational units of the company. Continuous improvement aiming at better usage of resources and limitation of the so-called bottlenecks. |
| Lean Management | Changes included adjusting the number of people employed to the needs, and choosing employees with proper experience and education to their position |
| -SMED | Rationalization of production and its efficiency |
| -Six Sigma | Introduction and adjustment of ERP systems for better company management |
| -Heijunka | Minimizing the inventory level without loss for customers |

Source: Author's own analysis based on Wratislavia-Bio Sp. z o.o.'s financial data.

Applied changes specified in the restructuring process allowed to achieve measurable effects (Table 72) in the form of stable functioning of the company and a positive net result visible after the first six months from introducing changes. The liquidity (Table 72) significantly improved. The company debt was subject to gradual limitation, and the debt ratio in 2014 amounted to 54%, so it was slightly below the range determined as a norm in literature (57–67%). The turnover and profitability ratios after restructuring were on an acceptable, correct level. It is important to mention net working capital, which, in spite of good results achieved every year, is negative, which shows that there are significant liabilities as compared to the company property. Apart from that, the Altman's model significantly improved, and its result is slightly below the border level dividing companies functioning correctly from those at risk. The other ratios were used to complement this analysis, and based on that, it can be claimed that the company was restructured in a proper way.

**Table 72. Financial ratios in Wratislavia-Bio Sp. z. o.o. before and after restructuring in 2008-2014**

| **Ratio name** | **Calculation method** | **Before Restructuring** | | | **During Restructuring** | | | **After Restructuring** |
|---|---|---|---|---|---|---|---|---|
| **Liquidity ratios** | | | | | | | | |
| **Ratio name** | **Calculation method** | **2008** | **2009** | **2010** | **2011** | **2012** | **2013** | **2014** |
| Current ratio | Current assets/Short-term liabilities | 0.64 | 0.74 | 0.17 | 0.14 | 0.62 | 0.88 | 0.77 |
| Quick ratio | (Current assets-Inventories–Prepayments)/ Short-term liabilities | 0.14 | 0.58 | 0.06 | 0.07 | 0.52 | 0.63 | .62 |
| Cash to debt ratio | Short-term investments/ Short-term liabilities | 0.00 | 0.14 | 0.02 | 0.02 | 0.08 | 0.10 | 0.17 |
| **Debt ratios** | | | | | | | | |
| **Ratio name** | **Calculation method** | **2008** | **2009** | **2010** | **2011** | **2012** | **2013** | **2014** |
| Debt ratio | Total liabilities/Total assets | 0.96 | 0.78 | 0.67 | 0.77 | 0.84 | 0.70 | 0.54 |
| Debt to equity ratio | Total liabilities/Equity | 121.40 | 3.66 | 2.17 | 3.48 | 5.79 | 2.48 | 1.25 |
| Long term debt to equity | Long-term liabilities/Equity | 47.16 | 47.54 | 1.68 | 0.00 | 0.00 | 1.04 | 0.00 |
| Fixed assets debt ratio | Tangible current assets/Long-term liabilities | 1.66 | 1.90 | 2.27 | | | 2.01 | |
| **Turnover ratios** | | | | | | | | |
| **Ratio name** | **Calculation method** | **2008** | **2009** | **2010** | **2011** | **2012** | **2013** | **2014** |
| Asset turnover ratio | Net revenues from sale/Total assets | 1.20 | 2.40 | 0.95 | 0.36 | 2.67 | 3.40 | 2.64 |
| Receivables turnover ratio | Net revenues from sale/Total receivables | 14.68 | 13.14 | 104.88 | 9.27 | 7.13 | 15.75 | 11.03 |
| Days sales outstanding | Total receivables*360/Net revenues from sale | 24.52 | 27.39 | 3.43 | 38.85 | 50.50 | 22.86 | 32.63 |
| Inventory turnover ratio | Net revenues from sale/Inventory | 4.11 | 35.25 | 34.18 | 6.90 | 33.89 | 34.67 | 33.77 |
| Days inventory turnover ratio | Inventory*360/Net revenues from sale | 87.51 | 10.21 | 10.53 | 52.21 | 10.62 | 10.38 | 10.66 |

**Table 72. (Continued)**

| Ratio name | Calculation method | Before Restructuring | | | During Restructuring | | | After Restructuring |
|---|---|---|---|---|---|---|---|---|
| | | **2008** | **2009** | **2010** | **2011** | **2012** | **2013** | **2014** |
| Days liabilities turnover ratio | Short-term liabilities*360/ Net revenues from sale | 176.19 | 63.05 | 95.75 | 763.83 | 112.83 | 43.00 | 73.59 |
| Cash ratio | Days receivables turnover ratio + days cycle of inventory – days liability turnover ratio | -64.15 | -25.45 | -81.79 | -672.77 | -51.70 | -9.76 | -30.30 |
| **Profitability ratios** | | | | | | | | |
| **Ratio name** | **Calculation method** | **2008** | **2009** | **2010** | **2011** | **2012** | **2013** | **2014** |
| Return on sales | Net income/Net revenue from sales | -0.14 | 0.01 | -0.28 | -0.78 | 0.06 | 0.03 | 0.06 |
| Return on assets | Net income/Total assets | -0.16 | 0.03 | -0.26 | -0.28 | 0.15 | 0.10 | 0.15 |
| Return on equity | Net income/Equity | -20.56 | 0.14 | -0.85 | -1.28 | 1.07 | 0.36 | 0.35 |
| Return on investment | Operating result/ Total assets | -0.10 | 0.08 | -0.19 | -0.26 | 0.22 | 0.21 | 0.25 |
| **Analysis of capital and property structure** | | | | | | | | |
| **Ratio name** | **Calculation method** | **2008** | **2009** | **2010** | **2011** | **2012** | **2013** | **2014** |
| Golden rule of balance sheet | (KW/AT)x100% | 0.01 | 0.31 | 0.32 | 0.25 | 0.30 | 0.44 | 0.74 |
| Silver rule of balance sheet | (KS/AT)x100% | 0.61 | 0.83 | 0.76 | 0.25 | 0.30 | 0.90 | 0.74 |

| Ratio name | Calculation method | Before Restructuring | | | During Restructuring | | | After Restructuring |
|---|---|---|---|---|---|---|---|---|
| | | 2008 | 2009 | 2010 | 2011 | 2012 | 2013 | 2014 |
| KON = Constant capital-fixed assets | | -36 726.30 | -15 043.40 | -18 403.40 | -55 861.00 | -60 051.00 | -9 206.64 | -21 997.56 |
| KON to total assets | (KON/Total assets) x 100% | -0.24 | -0.12 | -0.23 | -0.67 | -0.34 | -0.06 | -0.15 |
| KON to inventory and receivables | (KON/Inventory + Receivables) x 100% | -0.64 | -0.47 | -6.13 | -7.36 | -0.74 | -0.21 | -0.48 |
| **Altman's model – a model for developing markets** | | | | | | | | |
| **Ratio name** | **Calculation method** | **2008** | **2009** | **2010** | **2011** | **2012** | **2013** | **2014** |
| Altman's model for developing markets | EM score = 6.56 X1 + 3.26 X2 + 6.72 X3 + 1.05 X 4 + 3.35 | 0.47 | 3.43 | 0.10 | -3.52 | 3.23 | 5.02 | 5.29 |
| X1 | KON/Total assets | -0.24 | -0.12 | -0.23 | -0.67 | -0.34 | -0.06 | -0.15 |
| X2 | Accumulated retained earnings/total assets | -0.16 | 0.03 | -0.26 | -0.28 | 0.15 | 0.10 | 0.15 |
| X3 | EBIT/total assets | -0.10 | 0.08 | -0.19 | -0.26 | 0.22 | 0.21 | 0.25 |
| X4 | Equity market value/ Debt book value | 0.01 | 0.27 | 0.46 | 0.29 | 0.17 | 0.40 | 0.80 |

Source: Author's own analysis based on Wratislavia-Bio Sp. z o.o.'s financial data.

## 3.5. Conclusion on the Case Study

Corporate restructuring is a popular form of introducing changes in business entities. It is important to perform the process of checking the business, economic, legal (due diligence) status of the company. The whole restructuring process should be planned based on such information, including all tasks and, what is crucial, the schedule of their execution. The control of the restructuring process means performing a comparative analysis of the real situation with a previously planned one. The analysis of the remaining deviations shows the efficiency and rate of performed actions. To a large extent, it depends on the type of restructuring, but the case study referred to a production company which, as a result of its past actions, had been forced to stop production due to the lack of contracts and the lack of capital necessary to conduct a business activity. An important advantage was the company property in the form of a production installation, which remained as its potential and allowed to plan and implement restructuring. The preparation of the restructuring plan took several months, and the time horizon of its execution was also several months. It took over six months to move from its implementation to the results in the form of achieving a positive net result. This stage was the most important – a foundation of the further operations of the company, showing that the restructuring plan was accurate. Then, further necessary changes and the actions from the restructuring plan were implemented, but, due to the improved financial situation, this implementation was possible earlier and gave better results than before. The restructuring process lasted from 2011 to 2013. In 2014, the company entered a period after restructuring which involved activity in stable internal conditions. Other elements gained importance, including competitive advantage, achieved margin on products, or the operating result and the net result. However, these were problems of a different type than the earlier ones, where the managers struggled with the excessive debt and the lack of financial liquidity.

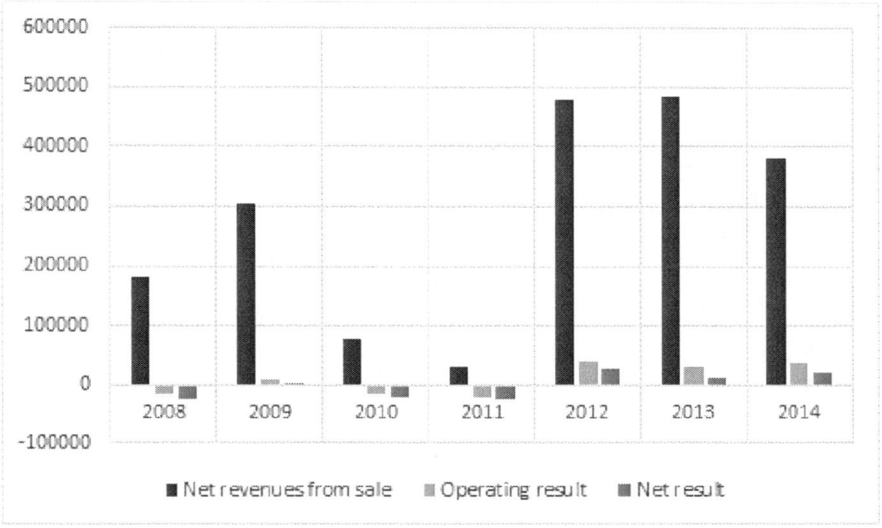


Source: Author's own analysis based on Wratislavia-Bio Sp. z o. o.'s financial data.

Figure 28. Financial results in Wratislavia-Bio Sp. zo.o. in 2008–2014 (PLN thousands)).

The restructuring process improved the situation of the company and improved its financial results (Figure 28). In 2014, net revenues were lower than the year before, but that was conditioned by the prices set at that time, the margin was kept on an acceptable level. The operating result and the net result were on a similar level as in the previous year. The positive effects of restructuring from 2014 allowed to prepare a strategy of company development, not only of keeping it on the market and supporting the functioning in a way it had been before. The actions were started to strengthen the company not only on national markets, but also abroad.

# CONCLUSION

Company owners and managers will aim at the development of their entities, as much as their competences and financial capacities allow. As a result, depending on the approach to risk, their actions will be more or less dynamic. The need to maintain or strengthen competitive advantage leads to the possibility to achieve better financial results and, consequently, may contribute to the increase in the company value. Thus, it is crucial to have a plan and aim at its execution. However, the situation is not always as the books present it, and the prepared plan is executed in accordance with the assumptions. Conducting a business activity may be surprising due to the changing conditions of functioning on different markets. Such a company can be compared to a ship which travels through the endless ocean waters. This entity has its own plan of actions, internal rules, and procedures which determine its strength and aim. However, the surrounding is crucial for the functioning of the company. The conducted activity is different when sailing on calm ocean waves, and different when dealing with a storm and breaking waves. It occurs that sometimes, even the most brilliant business ideas do not work. It is a great skill to be able to improve the company situation when facing approaching or occurring storm. Certain difficulties may arise if it occurs that previous business decision had been wrong. Then, a ship called "a company" starts to take on water, and the mountainous waves, understood as a quickly changing company environment, may lead to a very difficult situation of the company or even its bankruptcy. It is a difficult task to improve the situation and restore balance and stabilization. It can be achieved by company restructuring, which can take place when the company is in a critical condition and radical internal changes are necessary to remedy the situation. Restructuring can also be a method of increasing the efficiency of functioning. Thus, restructuring is related to revolutionary changes in companies and used in individual companies, but also in capital groups. In the latter case, restructuring aims at streamlining company functioning and improving the supervision, especially when the company operates globally.

This monograph presents restructuring as a tool to remedy company critical situation of excessive debt and improper use of its business model, which led to a dramatic decrease of revenues from sales and of financial results. At certain point, the presented company stopped operating because its activity was not profitable; the company had no contracts signed with any customers, generated net losses, and did not pay its bank credit. It was necessary to perform restructuring or declare bankruptcy. The company made a decision to perform restructuring which was prepared and planned in detail. The planned tasks were performed as per the schedule. Real changes were observed; any deviations from the plan were reported. The implementation and execution of the plan took more than a year, leading to the company restoring its financial and business balance. It should be emphasized that the company had a property of a production installation which constituted its potential but also a challenge, as it was crucial to use it in a proper way. It was crucial to prepare and apply a properly selected business model. It was also important to obtain capital necessary to start previously stopped operations and production, as well as to find first customers. Proper supervision and control over key indicators at the initial stage allowed to achieve a satisfying margin and restore financial liquidity over several months. Regained liquidity was a foundation and a driving force for further development. After this period, the company started a process of limiting its debt which existed due to previous negligence. The company aimed at increasing its efficiency by properly using its potential of the installation production and increasing sales, but also by maintaining or increasing the unit margin. What is more, apart from selling in Poland, the company could also compete on the European market. Before restructuring, all ratios were on inaccessible levels and indicated that the company was in a poor situation. After implementing the restructuring actions, the situation was improving and the ratios reached higher levels, though they were not always satisfactory. Even after restructuring, the level of the Z-score model was slightly below the norm. Thus, analysing the company, it is important to analyze the whole functioning, and not only its selected elements. Only such an approach guarantees proper evaluation of the company. In this case, the restructuring process was a success, but if the negligence was slightly more serious, this process could not have been conducted. It is important to make a decision about restructuring, but this process requires time from making a decision to its effects, and not every company can survive until the time of achieving the results of re-structuring. Due to the increasing competition and accumulation of capital, restructuring is going to be performed in companies all over the world, and a proper plan and the selection of restructuring tools and methods can be the last chance to save such companies or improve their efficiency. Restructuring is a difficult and arduous process which requires a lot of patience, but it is not impossible to execute.

# BIBLIOGRAPHY

Acocella N. 2002. *Zasady polityki gospodarczej.* [The rules of economic policy] Warszawa: PWN.

Bednarczyk M. 1994. *Zastosowane koncepcji spin off w przekształceniach przedsiębiorstw państwowych.* [The applied spin off concept in transformations of state-owned enterprises.] Zeszyty Naukowe AE Kraków, no. 444,

Bednarek M. 2007. *Doskonalenie systemów zarządzania, nowa droga do przedsiębiorstwa lean.* [Improving management systems, a new way to lean.] Difin, Warszawa.

Bednarski L. 2000. *Analiza finansowa w przedsiębiorstwie.* [Financial analysis in the enterprise] PWE, Warszawa.

Bieniok H., Marek J. 1999. *Kompleksowa metoda diagnozowania systemu zarządzania przedsiębiorstwa.* [A comprehensive method of diagnosing the enterprise's management system] AE, Katowice.

Bitkowska A. 2010. Przebieg procesu restrukturyzacji przedsiębiorstwa. [The course of the enterprise restructuring process.] [In:] Bitkowska A. (ed.). *Procesy restrukturyzacji warunkiem poprawy konkurencyjności przedsiębiorstw.* Difin, Warszawa.

Bitkowska A., Wójcik G., Kolterman K. 2010. Koncepcje restrukturyzacji przedsiębiorstw. [Concepts of enterprise restructuring.] In: Bitkowska

A. (ed.). *Procesy restrukturyzacji warunkiem poprawy konkurencyjności przedsiębiorstw*. Difin, Warszawa.

Borowiecki R. 1996. Analiza ekonomiczna jako narzędzie określania obszaru i zakresu działań restrukturyzacyjnych w przedsiębiorstwie. [Economic analysis as a tool for determining the area and scope of restructuring activities in an enterprise.] In: R. Borowiecki (ed.). *Restrukturyzacja w procesie przekształceń i rozwoju przedsiębiorstwa*. Kraków.

Borowiecki R., Nalepka A. 2003. Restrukturyzacja w procesie funkcjonowania i rozwoju przedsiębiorstw. [Restructuring in the process of functioning and development of enterprises.] In: Borowiecki R. (ed.). *Zarządzanie restrukturyzacją procesów gospodarczych. Aspekt teoretyczny–praktyczny*. Difin, Warszawa.

Borowiecki R., Wysłocka E. 2012. *Analiza ekonomiczna i ocena ekspercka w procesie restrukturyzacji przedsiębiorstw*. [Economic analysis and expert assessment in the process of enterprise restructuring.] Difin, Warszawa.

Brake T., Walker D. 1995. *Doing business internationally. The workbook to cross – cultural success*. Princeton, Training Management Corporation.

Buczkowska A. 2012. Cele przedsiębiorstwa a pomiar jego dokonań. [The goals of the company and the measurement of its achievements] In: *Zeszyty naukowe Uniwersytetu Szczecińskiego*, no. 684. *Finanse, rynki finansowe, ubezpieczenia*, no. 45.

Chabiera J., Doroszewicz S., Zbierzchowska A. 2000. *Zarządzanie jakością. Poradnik menedżera*. [Quality management. Manager's guide.] Centrum Informacji Menedżera, Warszawa.

Ciesielska D. 2009. *Offshoring usług. Wpływ na rozwój przedsiębiorstwa*. [Offshoring services. Impact on the development of the enterprise.] Wolters Kluwer Polska, Warszawa.

Copeland T., Koller T., Murrin J. *Wycena: mierzenie i kształtowanie wartości firm*. [Valuation: measuring and shaping the value of companies.] WIG-Press, Warszawa 197.

Crosby P. 1979. *Quality is Free: The Art. Of Making Quality Certain*. McGraw-Hill.

Ćwiąkała-Małys A., Nowak W. 2005. *Zarys metodologiczny analizy finansowej*. [Methodological outline of financial analysis.] Uniwersytet Wrocławski, Wrocław.

Czerska J. 2000. *Lean Production - konieczność, czy możliwość*. [Lean Production - a necessity or an opportunity] Manager 2000, no. 2.

Czyż-Gwiazda E. 2006. *Benchmarking. Benchmark Index czyli jak porównywać się z najlepszymi*? [Benchmarking. Benchmark Index - how to compare with the best?] Centrum Benchmarkingu Polska – TÜV NORD Polska Sp. z o.o., Katowice.

Dahlagaard J. J., Kristesen K., Kanji G. K. 2000. *Podstawy zarządzania jakością*. [Basics of quality management.] Wydawnictwo Naukowe PWN, Warszawa.

Damodaran A. 2002. *Estimating Risk Parameters*. Working paper, Stern School of Business, New York. Working paper, Stern Business School, New York University, http://pages.stern.nyu.edu/~adamodar.

Dichtl E., Issing O. 1984. *Exporte als Herausforderung fur die deutsche Wirtschaft*. [Exports as a challenge for the German economy.] Deutscher InstituteVerlang, Kol.

Dorozik G. 2006. Identyfikacja czynników prowadzących do sytuacji kryzysowych podmiotów gospodarczych. [Identification of factors leading to crisis situations of business entities.] In: L. Dorozik (ed.). R*estrukturyzacja ekonomiczna przedsiębiorstw w świetle polskiego prawa upadłościowego i naprawczego*. PWE, Warszawa.

Dudycz T. 2005. *Zarządzanie wartością przedsiębiorstwa*. [Enterprise value management.] PWE, Warszawa.

Duraj J. 2000. *Podstawy ekonomiki przedsiębiorstwa*. [Basics of enterprise economics.] PWE, Warszawa.

Dylewski M., Filipiak B., Szczypta P. 2010. *Budżetowanie w przedsiębiorstwie. Aspekty rachunkowe, finansowe i zarządcze*. [Budgeting in the enterprise. Accounting, financial and management aspects.] Cedewu, Warszawa.

Epstein R. C. Industrial Profits in 1917. *The Quarterly Journal of Economics*, 39(2).

Feigenbaum A. V. 1961. *Total Quality Control.* New York, McGraw-Hill.

Fijałkowska J. 2013. VAIC™ jako metoda pomiaru dokonań przedsiębiorstw. *Zarządzanie i Finanse 11.1* [Management and Finance 11.1], p. 2. Uniwersytet Gdański, Gdańsk.

Filipczuk J. 2004. *Analiza strategiczna przedsiębiorstwa, Teoria i praktyka.* [Strategic analysis of the company, theory and practice.] WSZiM, Sochaczew.

Fisher I. *The Theory of Interest.* The MacMillan Company, New York.

Gabrusewicz W. 1999. *Restrukturyzacja przedsiębiorstw i metody oceny jej efektów.* [Restructuring of enterprises and methods of assessing its effects.] Przegląd Organizacji 3/1999.

Gabrusiewicz W. 2002. *Podstawy analizy finansowej.* [Basics of financial analysis.] PWE, Warszawa.

Gajdzik B. 2012. *Restrukturyzacja przedsiębiorstw w warunkach destabilizacji otoczenia na przykładzie branży hutniczej.* [Restructuring of enterprises in conditions of destabilizing the environment on the example of the steel industry.] Difin, Warszawa.

Garbarski L. 1992. *Marketing.* PWE, Warszawa.

Garstka M. 2012. *Restrukturyzacja przedsiębiorstwa – podział przez wydzielenie.* [Enterprise restructuring - division by separation.] 2nd ed. Cedewu, Warszawa.

Gianakis G. A., McCue C. P. 1999. *Local Government Budgeting*, Praeger.

Gierszewska G., Romanowska M. 2003. *Analiza strategiczna przedsiębiorstwa.* [Strategic analysis of the company.] PWN, Warszawa.

Goetzman W. N., S. J. Garstka. 1999. The Development of Corporate Performance Measures: Benchmarks before EVA™. Yale ICF Working Paper 99-06, http://dx.doi.org/10.2139/ssrn.170674.

Gołębiowski G. Szczepankowski P. 2007. *Analiza wartości przedsiębiorstwa.* [Analysis of the enterprise value.] Difin, Warszawa.

Gołębiowski G., Tłaczała A. 2009. *Analiza finansowa w teorii i w praktyce.* [Financial analysis in theory and practice.] Difin, Warszawa.

Gołębiowski T. 2001. *Zarządzanie strategiczne, planowanie i kontrola.* [Strategic management, planning and control.] Difin, Warszawa.

Gordon M. J. *The Savings, Investment and Valuation of a Corporation.* The Review of Economics and Statistics 44:1.

Greaver M. F. 1999. *Strategic Outsourcing. A Structural Approach to Outsourcing Decisions and Initiatives.* Amacom, New York.

Griffin R. W. 2000. *Podstawy zarządzania organizacjami.* [Basics of organization management.] PWN, Warszawa.

Grudzewski W. M., Hejduk I. K. 2004. *Metody projektowania systemów zarządzania.* [Methods of designing management systems.] Difin, Warszawa.

Hamrol A., Mantura W. 1998. *Zarządzanie jakością. Teoria i praktyka.* [*Zarządzanie jakością. Teoria i praktyka.*] Wydawnictwo Naukowe PWN, Warszawa – Poznań.

Helfert A. E. 2004. *Techniki analizy finansowej.* [Techniques of financial analysis.] PWE, Warszawa.

Hempenstall E. 1999. *Being Successful in Budgeting.* Blackhall Publishing, Dublin.

Hernandez S. R., Kaluzny A. D. 2000. Innowacje i zmiany organizacyjne. [Innovations and organizational changes.] In: S. M. Shortell, A. D. Kaluzny. *Podstawy zarządzania opieką zdrowotną.* Versalius, Kraków.

Hirschleifer J. On the Theory of Optimal Investment Decision. *The Journal of Political Economy*, 66 (4).

Jablonski M. 2017. Methods of Evaluating the Investment Attractiveness of Business Models in the Context of the Performance Management Concept, [In:] M. Jablonski, *Strategic Performance Management: New Concepts and Contemporary Trends.* New York: Nova Science Publishers: 1-18.

Jaki A. 2008. Zarządzanie wartością – pomiar i ocena kreowania wartości. [Value management - measurement and evaluation of value creation] *Świat Nieruchomości* no. 64, 2008..

Jaki A. 2012. *Mechanizmy procesu zarządzania wartością przedsiębiorstwa.* [Mechanisms of enterprise value management process] UE, Kraków.

Jaki A. 2013. Pomiar i ocena efektywności kreowania wartości w przedsiębiorstwie. [Measurement and assessment of the effectiveness of creating value in an enterprise] *Finanse, Rynki Finansowe, Ubezpieczenia* no. 59 (760), Szczecin.

Kaczorowski P., Stępniak-Kucharska A. 1999. Próba oszacowania taksonomicznego wskaźnika restrukturyzacji. [An attempt to estimate the taxonomic index of restructuring.] *Working Papers* no. 16, INE PAN, Warszawa.

Karlof B., Stblom S. 1995. *Benchmarking – równaj do najlepszych.* [Benchmarking - equal to the best.] Biblioteka Menedżera i Bankowca, Warszawa.

Kawiński P. 2010. Restrukturyzacja pionu bankowości detalicznej PKO Banku Polskiego SA. [. Restructuring of the retail banking division of PKO Bank Polski SA.] In: Bitkowska A. (ed.). *Procesy restrukturyzacji warunkiem poprawy konkurencyjności przedsiębiorstw.* Difin, Warszawa.

Koch R. 1998. *Strategia.* [Strategy.] PWSB, Kraków.

Kolterman K. 2008. Lean production. *Ekonomika i organizacja przedsiębiorstwa* no. 4,

Kolterman K., Restrukturyzacja poprzez transfer technologii na przykładzie PHPU Arkol sp. z o.o.. [Restructuring through technology transfer on the example of PHPU Arkol sp. o.o.] In: Bitkowska A. 2010. (ed.) *Procesy restrukturyzacji warunkiem poprawy konkurencyjności przedsiębiorstw.* Difin, Warszawa.

Kortan J. ed. 2009. *Innowacje w strategii rozwoju organizacji w Unii Europejskiej.* [Innovations in the organization's development strategy in the European Union.] Difin, Warszawa.

Koźmiński A., W. Piotrowski, 2002. *Zarządzanie. Teoria i praktyka.* [Management. Theory and practice.] PWN, Warszawa.

Krajewski S., Kaczorowski P. Taksonomiczny wskaźnik restrukturyzacji. [Taxonomic restructuring ratio.] *Working Papers,* no. 27, INE PAN.

Krawiec F. 2005. Transformacja firmy w nowej gospodarce. *Koncepcje, strategie, struktury, struktury i technologie w zarządzaniu.* [Concepts, strategies, structures, structures and technologies in management] Difin.

Krishnamurti C., Vishwanath S. R. 2008. *Mergers, Acquisitions and Corporate Restructuring*. Business Books from SAGE, London.

Kulawik J., ed. 2008. *Analiza efektywności ekonomicznej i finansowej przedsiębiorstw rolnych powstałych na bazie majątku WRSP*. [Analysis of economic and financial efficiency of agricultural enterprises created on the basis of WRSP assets.] Warszawa.

Kuryłek Z. 2017. *Wykup lewarowany. Sposób akwizycji firm.* [Leveraged buyout. Way of acquiring companies.] Difin, Warszawa.

Kuryłek Z. 2015. Mezzanine Capital. *Nowoczesne finansowanie przedsiębiorstw,* CeDeWu, Warszawa.

Lichtarski J. 2001. *Podstawy nauki o przedsiębiorstwie.* [Basics of enterprise science.] AE, Wrocław.

Lichtarski J., ed. 2003. *Podstawy nauki o przedsiębiorstwie.* [Basics of enterprise science.] AE Wrocław.

Luque-Martınez Munoz T., Leiva F. 2005. *City Benchmarking: A Methodological Proposal Referring Specifically to Granada*, "Cities", Vol. 22, No. 6, 2005.

Malara Z. 2001. *Restrukturyzacja organizacyjna przedsiębiorstwa.* [Organizational restructuring of the enterprise.] Oficyna Wydawnicza Politechniki Wrocławskiej, Wrocław.

Malinowska M., Kucharska B., ed. 2006. *Zachowania podmiotów rynkowych w warunkach globalizacji.* [Behaviors of market entities in the conditions of globalization.] PWE, Warszawa.

Marecki K. 2002. *Rachunkowość menedżerska w gospodarce finansowej przedsiębiorstwa.* [Managerial accounting in the financial management of an enterprise.] 2nd edition. Wyd. Difin, Warszawa.

Maśloch P. 2011. *Restrukturyzacja przedsiębiorstw w Polsce w dobie transformacji i globalizacji*, [Restructuring of enterprises in Poland in the era of transformation and globalization] WSB Toruń, Toruń.

Mioduchowska-Jaroszewicz E. 2012. *Ocena przepływów pieniężnych w grupach kapitałowych.* [Assessment of cash flows in capital groups.]

Zeszyty Naukowe Uniwersytetu Szczecińskiego. Finanse. Rynki finansowe. Ubezpieczenia 56.

Motylska – Kuźma A. Wieprow J. 2017. *Psychologiczne aspekty podejmowania decyzji finansowych w przedsiębiorstwie* [Psychological aspects of making financial decisions in the enterprise], Szczecin, Zeszyty Naukowe Uniwersytetu Szczecińskiego, Finanse, Rynki Finansowe, Ubezpieczenia nr 1/2017 (85): 129-139.

Motylska – Kuźma, A. 2018. Alternative finance and sustainable development. *The Central European Review of Economics and Management*, 2(1): 175-187.

Mozalewski M. 2010. Rodzaje i metody restrukturyzacji przedsiębiorstw. [Types and methods of enterprise restructuring.] *Ruch Prawniczy, Ekonomiczny i Socjologiczny*, no. 2, UE Poznań, p. 216, R. Borowiecki. 2014. *Zarządzanie restrukturyzacją przed-siębiorstw i gospodarki*. Fundacja UE Kraków, Kraków, p. 14–18.

Nalepka A. 1999. *Restrukturyzacja przedsiębiorstwa. Zarys problematyki.* [Company restructuring. Outline of the problem.] PWN, Warszawa.

Nazarko J., Kuźmicz K., Szubzda E., Urban J. 2008. Ogólna koncepcja benchmarkingu i jego stosowalność w szkolnictwie wyższym. [The general concept of benchmarking and its applicability in higher education.] In: *Benchmarking w systemie szkolnictwa wyższego.* Woźnicki J. (ed.). 2008. Fundacja Rektorów Polskic*h*, Warszawa.

Nita B. 2014. *Niefinansowy pomiar dokonań przedsiębiorstw produkcyjnych w teorii i praktyce*. [Non-financial measurement of the achievements of manufacturing enterprises in theory and practice] Prace UE, UE Wrocław no. 335, Wrocław.

Oleksiuk A., J. 2013. Białek, *Mikroekonomia*, (ebook). KeyText.

Olszewski S. 2010. Restrukturyzacja procesów na przykładzie Biura Projektów Telekomunikacyjnych [Process restructuring on the example of Telecommunications Project Office], In: Bitkowska A. (ed.). *Procesy restrukturyzacji warunkiem poprawy konkurencyjności przed-siębiorstw.* Difin, Warszawa.

Osbert–Pociecha G. 2007. Relacja między efektywnością i elastycznością organizacji. [Relation between the efficiency and flexibility of the organization.] In: *Efektywność - Rozważania nad istotą i pomiarem,* (ed.) Dudycz T., Tomaszewicz Ł. AE Wrocław, Wrocław 2007.

Otley D. 2006. Measuring Performance: The Accounting Perspective. In: A. Neely (ed.). *Business Performance Measurement. Theory and practice*, Cambridge University Press, Cambridge.

Pasternak K., Grzybowska B. 2000. *Metody i techniki zarzadzania w przedsiębiorstwie*. [Methods and techniques of management in the enterprise.] Wydawnictwo Uniwersytetu Warmińsko–Mazur-skiego, Olsztyn.

Pastuszak Z. 1999. *Restrukturyzacyjne skutki prywatyzacji przedsiębiorstw państwowych. Technika, produkcja, logistyka.* [Restructuring effects of privatization of state-owned enterprises. Technology, production, logistics.] Politechnika Lubelska, Lublin.

Penc J. 1997. *Strategie zarządzania, perspektywiczne myślenie, systemowe działanie*. [Management strategies, forward thinking, systemic action.] Placet, Warszawa.

Pernsteiner H., and Węcławski J. 2017. Factors of Influence on Relationship Banking of Polish Firms. In: Jajuga K., Orlowski L., Staehr K. (eds.). *Contemporary Trends and Challenges in Finance.* Springer 2017 *Proceedings in Business and Economics*: 203-211.

Pierścionek Z. 1995. *Zarządzanie strategiczne w przedsiębiorstwie.* [Strategic management in the enterprise] Oficyna Wydawnicza SGH, Warszawa.

Pierścionek Z. 1996. Restrukturyzacja, a rozwój i strategie przedsiębiorstw. [Restructuring, and the development and strategies of enterprises.] In: *Restrukturyzacja w procesie przekształceń i rozwoju przedsiębiorstw*. AE Kraków, TNOiK: 1996,

Piwowar A. 2015. Produkcja biokomponentów i biopaliw ciekłych w Polsce – tendencje rozwoju i regionalne zróżnicowanie. [Production of biocomponents and liquid biofuels in Poland - tendencies of development and regional differentiation.] In: *Roczniki Naukowe Stowarzyszenia Ekonomistów Rolnictwa i Agrobiznesu* XVII, volume 2. Warszawa.

Porada-Rochoń M., ed. 2009. *Restrukturyzacja przedsiębiorstw w procesie adaptacji do współczesnego otoczenia.* [Restructuring of enterprises in the process of adaptation to the contemporary environment] Difin, Warszawa.

Porter M. E. 1998. Choix strategiques et concurrence. [Strategic choice and competition] *Ekonomica*, Paryż.

Relich. M. 2015. A computational intelligence approach to predicting new product success. *Proceedings of the 11th International Conference on Strategic Management and its Support by Information Systems*: 142-150.

Rojek T. 2016. Wykorzystanie narzędzi restrukturyzacji w procesie zarządzania efektywnością przedsiębiorstwa. [The use of restructuring tools in the process of enterprise performance management] *Studia Oeconomica Posnaniensia*, v. 4, no. 2. UE Poznań.

Rue L., Holland P. 1989. *Strategic Management.* Mc Graw-Hill New York.

Rutkowska A., Teoretyczne aspekty efektywności – pojęcie i metody pomiaru [Theoretical aspects of efficiency - the concept and methods of measurement], *Zarządzanie i Finanse*, nr 1, cz. 4, Uniwersytet Gdański, Gdańsk 2013,

Rydzewska-Włodarczyk M., Sobieraj M. 2015. Pomiar efektywności procesów za pomocą kluczowych wskaźników efektywności. [Measuring the effectiveness of processes using key performance indicators.] *Zeszyty Naukowe Uniwersytetu Szczecińskiego* no. 864. Finanse, Rynki Finansowe, Ubezpieczenia no. 76 v. 2, Szczecin.

Samuelson P. A., Nordhaus W. D. 2007. *Ekonomia.* [Economy] PWN, v. 1, Warszawa.

Sapijaszka Z. 1997. *Restrukturyzacja przedsiębiorstwa. Szanse i ograniczenia.* [Company restructuring. Chances and limitations.] PWN, Warszawa.

Sashkin M., Kiser K.J. 1993. Putting Total Quality Management to Work. Berret-Koehler Publisher, San Francisco, p. 39. J. J. Bonstingl. 1995. *Szkoły jakości, Wprowadzenie do Total Quality Management w edukacji.* CODN, Warszawa.

Sawicki K., ed. 2001. *Polityka bilansowa i analiza finansowa. Nowoczesne instrumenty zarządzania firmą.* [Balance sheet policy and financial analysis. Modern instruments of company management.] Wyd. Ekspert, Wrocław.

Sierpińska M., Jachna T. 2004. *Ocena przedsiębiorstwa wg. standardów światowych.* [Company rating by global standards.] PWN, Warszawa.

Skrzypek E. 2007. Efektywność ekonomiczna jako ważny czynnik sukcesu organizacji. [Economic efficiency as an important factor in organizational success.] In: T. Dudycz, G. Osbert-Pociecha, B. Brycz (ed.). *Efektywność – konceptualizacja i uwarunkowania.* Prace Naukowe Uniwersytetu Ekonomicznego we Wrocławiu no. 262. Wydawnictwo UE we Wrocławiu, Wrocław.

Slatter S., Lovett D. 2001. *Restrukturyzacja firmy. Zarządzanie przedsiębiorstwem w sytuacjach kryzysowych.* [Company restructuring. Business management in crisis situations.] WIG-Press, Warszawa.

Sloan L. H., *Corporate Profits, A Study of Their Size, Variation, Use and Distribution in a Period of Prosperity*, Harper and Brothers Publishers, New York, 1929,

Śnieżek E. 2008. *Jak korzystać z rachunku przepływów pieniężnych.* [How to use the cash flow statement.] Rachunkowość no. 1.

Solomons D. 1963. *Divisional Performance: Measurement and Control.* Financial Executives, New York.

Source – Loda M. 2014. *Benchmarking – nowoczesna koncepcja zarządzania organizacją.* [Benchmarking - a modern concept of organization management.] Prace Naukowo-Dydaktyczne PWSZ im. S. Pigonia w Krośnie Z. 67, Krosno.

Strahl D. 1990. *Metody programowania rozwoju społeczno-gospodarczego.* [Methods of programming socio-economic development.] PWE, Warszawa.

Suszyński C. 2003. *Restrukturyzacja, konsolidacja, globalizacja przedsiębiorstw. Doświadczenia i perspektywy polskiej transformacji.* [Restructuring, consolidation, globalization of enterprises. Experiences and perspectives of Polish transformation.] PWE, Warszawa.

Suszyński C. 2009. *Restrukturyzacja przedsiębiorstw*. [Restructuring of enterprises.] PWE, Warszawa.

Szucki T. 1998. *Encyklopedia marketingu*. [Encyclopedia of marketing.] Placet, Warszawa.

Szymańska E. 2010. Efektywność przedsiębiorstw – definiowanie i pomiar. [Enterprise efficiency - defining and measuring.] *Roczniki Nauk Rolniczych*. Seria G, Ekonomika Rolnictwa, V. 97, P. 2, Warszawa.

Thompson A., Srickland A. 1984. Strategic Management, Business Publications Inc., Piano, p. 80, qtd. in M. Garstka. 2012. *Restrukturyzacja przedsiębiorstwa – podział przez wydzielenie*, 2nd ed. Cedewu, Warszawa.

Trocki M. 2001. *Outsourcing. Metoda restrukturyzacji działalności gospodarczej*. [Outsourcing. Method of business restructuring.] PWE, Warszawa.

Walczak M. (ed.). 2003. *Analiza finansowa w zarządzaniu przedsiębiorstwem*. [Financial analysis in enterprise management.] Warszawa.

Węcławski J. 1997. *Venture Capital. Nowy instrument finansowania przedsiębiorstw*. PWN, Warszawa.

Węcławski J. 2006. Hybrydowe instrumenty finansowania przedsiębiorstw. [Hybrid financing instruments for enterprises.] In: *Finanse przedsiębiorstwa*. P. Karpuś (ed.). UMCS, Lublin.

Wędzki D. 2010. Wykorzystanie rachunku przepływów pieniężnych do analizy finansowej. [Use of the cash flow statement for financial analysis.] *„Rachunkowość”* 2010, no. 1.

Wilczyński R. Pomiar efektywności a cele przedsiębiorstw, [Measurement of effectiveness and goals of enterprises,] Zeszyty Naukowe Uniwersytetu Szczecińskiego no. 803. *„Finanse, Rynki Finansowe, Ubezpieczenia”* no. 66, Wydawnictwo Naukowe Uniwersytetu Szczecińskiego, Szczecin, www.wneiz.pl/frfu.

Wójcik G. 2010. Restrukturyzacja firmy szkoleniowej Centrum Edukacji EDUS. [Restructuring of the training company EDUS Education

Center.] In: Bitkowska A. (ed.). *Procesy restrukturyzacji warunkiem poprawy konkurencyjności przedsiębiorstw*, Difin, Warszawa 2010.

Wójcik K. A. 2010. Restrukturyzacja na przykładzie koncernu Volkswagen. [Restructuring on the example of Volkswagen.] In: Bitkowska A. (ed.). *Procesy restrukturyzacji warunkiem poprawy konkurencyjności przedsiębiorstw*, Difin, Warszawa.

Womack J. P., Jones D. T., Ross D. 2001. *The Machine that Changed the World: The Story of Lean Production*. Harper Collins.

Wysłocka E. 2004. Zarządzanie restrukturyzacja przedsiębiorstwa, a metody analizy ekonomicznej. [Business restructuring management, and methods of economic analysis.] In: Cz. Glinkowski (ed.). *Zarządzanie zmianą. Kierunki i efektywność restrukturyzacji sprywatyzowanych przedsiębiorstw w Polsce*. Warszawa.

Żurek J., ed. 2007. *Przedsiębiorstwo, Zasady działania, funkcjonowanie, rozwój*. [Enterprise, Operating principles, functioning, development.] Uniwersytet Gdański.

## OTHER SOURCES

Act of 25 August 2006 on biocomponents and liquid biofuels (Dz. U. [*Journal of Laws*] of 2006 No. 169 item 1199).

Act on biocomponents and liquid biofuels of 25 August 2006 (*Journal of Laws* of 2006 No. 169 item 1199).

Act on biocomponents and liquid biofuels of 25 August 2006 (*Journal of Laws No. 169 item 1199*, as amended), Regulation of the Council of Ministers of 13 August 2013 on National Index Targets for 2013-2018 (Dz. U. [Journal of Laws] of 2013, item 918), ARR's President's ordinance no. 173/2011/Z of 27 December 2011.

http://www.teraz-srodowisko.pl/aktualnosci/Szykuje-sie-rozwoj-biopaliw-wyzszej-generacji-1790.html, access: 24.11.2016.

Wratislavia-Bio Sp. z o.o.'s financial data www.nafta.wn.pl, access: 20.03.2017.

# About the Author

Zbigniew Kuryłek, PhD, is an Assistant Professor at WSB University in Wrocław. He obtained his doctorate in finance focusing on private equity investments using mezzanine capital. His research interests concern methods of corporates' financing and M&A transactions. Author of monographs, many articles, and a participant of international scientific conferences.

# INDEX

## C

## D



## E

## F



## G

## H



## I



## J



## K



## L

## Q



## R

## S



## T

## U



## V



## W



## Z